Preparing for Marriage

Preparing

for

Marriage

by
DR. JACK SCHAAP

Pastor
First Baptist Church of Hammond, Indiana

Hyles Publications
523 Sibley Street
Hammond, Indiana 46320

Dedication

This book is lovingly dedicated to that special group of teenagers who made Mrs. Schaap and me feel so welcome as their new pastor and wife.

I have referred to these young adults as my " '01'ers," for they were high school graduates in 2001, but they also represent that band of people who in 2001 had to say goodbye to their beloved pastor, Brother Hyles—the only pastor most of them had ever known—and transfer their love and loyalty to a new pastor.

I love you "kids" dearly, and you will always hold a special place in my heart!

Contents

Contents
(continued)

Preface

JACK SCHAAP ARRIVED at Hyles-Anderson College in January of 1977. Through some remarkable experiences, he met and began dating Cindy Hyles.

Brother Schaap graduated from Hyles-Anderson College in May of 1978 with his bachelor's degree. He received his master's degree in May of 1979. On June 1, 1979, Jack and Cindy were married by Cindy's father, Dr. Jack Hyles, at First Baptist Church of Hammond.

Brother Schaap began teaching Bible at Hyles-Anderson College in September of 1979. Five years later, he became an assistant to the president. In the spring of 1996, Dr. Schaap became the vice-president at Hyles-Anderson College.

On March 7, 2001, Dr. Schaap became the pastor of First Baptist Church of Hammond, Indiana. His greatest desire is to carry on and perpetuate the work of First Baptist Church of Hammond just like his father-in-law would have wanted it.

Dr. and Mrs. Schaap have two children. Their daughter, Jaclynn, 21, is a graduate of Hyles-Anderson College, and their son, Kenny, 17, is a senior at Hammond Baptist High School.

Brother Schaap has traveled extensively across America and has become one of America's foremost preachers. He has been a bus captain for 12 years, starting with one bus route with six riders. He now captains six bus routes, which had a high day of nearly 400.

In this book, Dr. Schaap presents a personal one-on-one session on premarital counseling. As a faculty member at Hyles-Anderson College, Brother Schaap counseled over 50 people a week. Many of these appointments centered on the subject of marriage. As pastor of First Baptist Church of Hammond, Indiana, Brother Schaap averages seeing and counseling over 150 people each week.

Introduction

IN SEPTEMBER OF 1979, I began teaching at Hyles-Anderson College. Four years later, I began a single, young-adult Sunday school class at First Baptist Church of Hammond. Through these many years now, I have been privileged to teach and to counsel many hundreds of couples as they began preparing for a wonderful adventure called marriage. I strongly and firmly recommend marriage. I highly believe in the institution of marriage, and I love being a married man.

I love to help, counsel, and instruct young couples as they begin their early days of dating. I love to watch them go through those wonderful days of courtship where they discover their love for one another, then share expressions and tokens of love, and ultimately share the presentation of an engagement ring. As each couple I counsel begins the preparations for the wedding day and begins to meet with me for premarital counseling, I get to know them better and have the privilege to assist them in preparing for a happy and blessed marriage. The following material is what I teach each couple who seeks counsel.

ONE

Building on a Solid Foundation

MARRIAGE WAS ORDAINED by God; therefore, the institution of marriage is good, wonderful, wholesome, and blessed. Because I am a firm believer in marriage, I recommend that a couple prepare diligently and thoroughly for their marriage prior to their wedding day. This preparation will provide a good, solid foundation for a happy marriage. Too many couples spend the majority of their time planning only for the wedding day. Of course, I am not minimizing the fact that there should be much preparation for that "crowning day" in a young lady's life. However, the wedding day is over very quickly; the expenses, the planning, the flowers, the attendants, and the meal quickly fade to memories in a photo album.

The marriage continues though, and, sad to say, many couples (if not most couples) fail to plan thoroughly for the marriage. If every couple would just plan for the marriage as thoroughly as they prepare for their wedding day, they could enjoy a wonderful start to that God-ordained blessed institution of marriage.

Normally, when I agree to counsel a couple, I set up four counseling sessions. Each one lasts one hour and a half. These counseling times start about six months before the wedding day. We meet approximately every six weeks and have our last session approximately one month before the date of the wedding. This schedule gives me time to assign the couple topics to discuss on their own, as well as recommending books for them to read. The next counseling session I spend part of the time asking and answering questions from the assignments. With the remaining time, I teach and help prepare them for their wedding day as well as for their marriage.

During our first session, I take time to get to know the couple. I interview them and ask questions about their individual backgrounds. I also ask how they met one another and how they became Christians. I personally do not believe that any marriage can be established and built on a solid foundation if both the husband and the wife are not born-again Christians who are living for the Lord.

Marriage is a picture of the relationship that the Lord Jesus Christ has with His bride, the local church. I believe that the husband-wife relationship is to be a testimony on this earth to show the love Jesus Christ has for us who believe in Him as our Saviour. Therefore, it is impossible to have a proper symbol of the love between Christ and His people if both of the engaged couple are not born-again Christians.

THE MOST IMPORTANT DECISION
A COUPLE CAN MAKE ABOUT MARRIAGE

Before I continue any further on the subject of preparing for marriage, I want to explain the importance of being a Christian and how to become a Christian.

God started the institution of marriage as a beautiful

earthly picture of what He had intended all along for Himself. At the beginning of the Bible in Genesis, God is alone. In Genesis 1:1 the Bible says, *"In the beginning God...,"* which indicates that He was alone. In Genesis 1:20, He created the animals. In Genesis 1:26, God created man, Adam. In Revelation, the last book of the Bible, God describes Himself with His bride or His wife, if you please, and He describes the beginning of a wonderful eternal relationship, a relationship built on depth of love, intimacy, and companionship. The Bible begins with God by Himself and ends with God and His wife. Greatly simplified, the Bible from Genesis 1:1 to Revelation 21:21 is the story of how God courts and marries His wife.

God is preparing His children for their eternal home in Heaven with Him, and He is preparing them to rule and reign on this earth with Him as His bride. He also allows us to enjoy on this earth that same beautiful, wonderful, blessed relationship (marriage) which pictures the relationship that He will someday have with His children. In other words, God has a man and his wife picture Himself and His bride.

> *"Since God ordained marriage, He alone has the right to make the rules."*

How difficult it would be to have God symbolized by a non-Christian man, and how poor a representation it would be if the bride (who is supposed to exemplify the child of God) would be less than a child of God! God says marriage is to be a symbolic picture of Himself and His bride. Practically speaking, the success of a marriage is contingent upon the husband and the wife understanding the marriage rules and the principles that God has given in His Book. God is building a marriage for Himself and since God ordained marriage, He alone has the right to make the rules. God alone knows the secrets to a happy and healthy marriage. Therefore, the single most important preparation for marriage is that both the bride-to-be and the husband-to-be understand what it is to be a Christian and what it is to be a good Christian at that.

To become a Christian, there are four simple facts from the Bible that one must know. First of all, God says that all men are sinners. I'm a sinner; you are a sinner. By birth, you and I inherited from our fathers a sin nature—a sin nature that will one day claim our physical life and bring death. The Bible says, *"...sin, when it is finished, bringeth forth death."* (James 1:15)

The reason everyone born into this world has died is that he, by birth, has been born a sinner. Sin manifests itself in many different ways. Some people are openly sinful with habits and practices that the majority of people would look upon with disdain. Some people are drunkards, drug addicts, rapists, child molesters, or violent murderers. Many of us sinners tend to be a little more careful in how we allow our sin to be revealed in our lives. Perhaps our sins are hidden in the heart and mind and are revealed in our motives.

Regardless of how our sins are exposed, we are sinners because of a sin nature passed on to us through our fathers. The Bible says in Romans 5:12, *"Wherefore, as by one man sin entered into the world, and death by sin; and so death passed upon all men, for that all have sinned."* I have sinned, and you have sinned; God declares all of us guilty of being sinners. The first of God's four points is that we are all sinners.

The second important point to understand is that there is a penalty on this sin nature. God says in Romans 6:23, *"For the wages of sin is death...."* This verse means that the payment or the result or the natural end of sin is death. That death spoken of in Romans 6:23 is not only a physical death; it is also a spiritual death. In Revelation 21:8, the Bible describes a *"second death"* as being not only the place where the body is sent to the grave, but also a place where the soul of man, *the real you*—the you that understands what I have written, the you who understands other humans in conversation—would be. It is a lake burning with fire and brimstone called the Lake of Fire which is the *"second death."* Of course, no one wants to go there.

In fact, the Bible teaches that the Lake of Fire was not prepared for man. The Bible teaches very clearly that the Lake of Fire was prepared for the angelic beings under the domain of Satan, who rebelled against God. If a person goes to Hell (the Lake of Fire), he would be going as an intruder or a trespasser. It has never been God's intention or God's desire that anyone should perish in Hell. In fact, the Bible very clearly states that *"The Lord is…not willing that any should perish, but that all should come to repentance."* (II Peter 3:9) God wants every person to be a Christian! His great desire is that no man would spend eternity in the Lake of Fire.

Let me review: (1) I am a sinner, and you are a sinner. The Bible says, *"For **all** have sinned."* (2) There is a penalty or a price on sin, and that penalty is death in Hell, the lake of fire. The third point that every person must understand in order to become a Christian is that Jesus Christ paid the sin debt. He paid the price for every man's sins. In so doing, He provided an escape from Hell for every sinner, and that escape is through His substitutionary death.

As a sinner, I should die someday, go to Hell, and be punished for my sins. However, Jesus Christ paid my price by the infinite and eternal sacrifice of His own life. He shed His precious blood on an old rugged cross nearly 2,000 years ago. Not only did He die on that cross, but He was buried, and three days later, He arose from the dead! That ascent of Christ from the grave is the one distinction that sets Christianity apart from every other world religion.

Many religions have wonderful, moral leaders, or great examples of self-discipline, but no religion other than Christianity has a resurrected Saviour. The song writer said,

I serve a risen Saviour, He's in the world today.

Praise God, the words of that song are true. Jesus Christ is alive, real, and living. He is not just an imaginary figure. Yes, He is a historical figure, but He is much more than that—He died, He was buried, He rose again, and He lives. I believe these facts with all of my heart, and I want you to believe them with all of your heart.

I want you to believe that (1) You are a sinner, (2) There is a price or a penalty on your sin which is death in Hell, and (3) Jesus Christ, the Son of God, was born of a virgin, lived a sinless life, and gave Himself willingly to die for you. The Bible says, *"For God so loved the world, that he gave his only begotten Son, that whosoever believeth in him should not perish, but have everlasting life."* (John 3:16) The Bible also says in Romans 5:8, *"...God commendeth his love toward us,"* or God revealed or proved His love toward us, *"...in that, while we were yet sinners, Christ died for us."*

Christ loved us and died for us because of that great love. The third fact we need to know is that Jesus Christ paid our sin debt and has thus made a way for us to escape the fires of Hell to become a Christian. That fact leads me to my fourth and final statement.

Every person must by faith receive Jesus Christ as his personal Saviour. In Romans 10:13 the Bible says, *"For whosoever shall call upon the name of the Lord shall be saved."* The Bible says in Romans 10:10, *"For with the heart man believeth unto righteousness; and with the mouth confession is made unto salvation."* Quite simply, what God is saying is, "I want you to believe in your heart that you are a sinner and that there is a price on sin. Jesus Christ paid that price, and I will save you if you want Me to." He also says, "I want you to say it with your lips. With your mouth, claim Jesus Christ as your Saviour. By faith, believe in Him as your Saviour." It is not enough to believe that He is a Saviour or that He was the Son of God; one must personally make Him his Saviour.

Let me explain. One day, when I was just a young boy, my older sister spoke with me at great length. She explained to me what I have just finished explaining to you. Though she was just a young girl herself, she knew that I was a sinner and that there was a price on my sin. She wanted me to understand that Jesus paid that price and that I had to personally receive Christ as my Saviour. I bowed my head in her presence, and with my own lips and in my own voice I said, "Dear God, I am a sinner. I know that. I believe there is a penalty on sin. I believe I deserve to die and go to Hell, but I don't want to go there. I want to be saved. I believe Jesus died for my sins and paid my price and died in my place. Jesus, I want You to come into my heart. I want You to be my Saviour. I want You to forgive me of my sin, and I want You to take me to Heaven when I die. I want to be a Christian."

In my heart I knew the Bible was right. I knew I was a sinner, and I knew Jesus Christ loved me and that He died on the cross for me. That day, by faith, I received Christ as my Saviour. That testimony shows exactly what it means to become a Christian.

At this moment, if you have not already done so, I invite you to do that. Let me ask you, my friend, do you believe that you are a sinner? Of course, you do. I am a sinner. I believe that fact, and I believe that you would also have to agree with me that you are a sinner. I don't mean that you have committed some horrible act. You may or may not have done so; however, that is not the issue. The issue is that every person has a sinful nature inside. Every person knows that it is much easier to do wrong than to do right. No person has ever had to be taught to cheat, to be dishonest, to lie, to stretch the truth, or to tell a white lie. Those urges and impulses toward wrong or improper thoughts come quite naturally.

By nature, you are a sinner, and you know that. My friend, you also know that the Bible is very clear about the price (or penalty) on sin. Even our society believes that if a person commits a crime, he must be punished. God, Who is the perfect Judge of the universe, has said that there is a penalty on sin.

Thirdly, isn't it wonderful news that Jesus loves every person? Because of that great love, He gave Himself for us, He died for us and rose again to save every person from his sin.

My friend, at this moment, wouldn't you like to bow your head right where you are? Regardless of where you are or who is with you, I want you to bow your head and by faith receive Jesus Christ into your heart as your personal Saviour.

Let me help you. Right now, would you pray this prayer:

> *Dear God, I am a sinner, and I am sorry for my sin. I believe there is a penalty on my sin. I deserve to die and go to Hell, but I don't want to do that. I want to go to Heaven when I die, and I believe Jesus Christ made a way for me to get to Heaven. Right now by faith, I receive Jesus Christ into my heart as my personal Saviour. Save me from my sin. Take me to Heaven when I die. Be my Saviour, Jesus, and thank You for Your forgiveness. Thank You for saving me. Thank You for making me one of Your own children. Amen."*

My friend, accepting Jesus as your personal Saviour is just the beginning of a wonderful life called Christianity. Being a happily married person means having a right relationship with the Author of marriage, the Founder of marriage, the Law-giver of marriage. Therefore, receiving Jesus Christ as your personal Saviour is critically important. I beg you to go back and reread this section again if it was not all perfectly clear in your mind. Read it again and again and again until the truth sinks into your heart and until you understand and obey the command of God to receive Jesus Christ as your Saviour. Truly salvation is the most important decision a person can make in his personal life.

～

Checklist and Review

1. Every couple should plan and prepare for their marriage just like they planned and prepared for their ___.

2. Each marriage is supposed to picture the relationship of Christ to ___, which is ___.

3. An unsaved person is a ___ symbol of this relationship.

4. Since marriage is established by God, then it makes sense to be a child of His through salvation in order to have His help in this institution called ___.

TWO

Choosing a Counselor

I WANT TO DISCUSS the importance of choosing a marriage counselor. Please read what follows carefully because I promise that I know what I am teaching. It has been my privilege, my delight, and my responsibility to have over 25,000 counseling sessions with young couples, young adults, married couples, and engaged couples on these very topics about which I am writing. Again and again, especially in the book of Proverbs, the Bible emphasizes the importance of seeking good advice.

I don't care who the person is or in what profession he is engaged. I don't care how many good marriages a person has witnessed through the years. At different times in married life when the marriage hits a snag, every person needs to seek counsel from a man of God or from some other wise man. In fact, a very wise couple contemplating marriage will choose a counselor because choosing the right counselor could prevent some of the major difficulties that cause divorce.

Oftentimes, a counselor can help solve a minor problem before it becomes a major problem. Counselors may prevent the little problems from escalating and developing into big problems.

The following is the way I suggest a couple should choose their counselor. Individually, each person should take out a sheet of paper or even use the margin of this book. Each person should list at least five but preferably ten names of men of God whom they trust. These names should be the names of proven men of God who have a sound record of possessing wisdom, knowledge, and understanding. Another factor to consider is whether or not these men of God can be reached for advice in a fairly short period of time.

Some ideal possibilities would be the pastor, a Christian schoolteacher, an assistant pastor, or a principal. (If you are a new Christian and if you don't know any people with whom you can counsel, you should consult with a good pastor, and he could give some suggestions.)

After thinking of the names, write them down in order of preference. Number one on the list should be the first choice, number two should be the second choice, etc. When each has finished writing his list, the couple should compare the two lists. The first name that appears on both lists is the person to circle on the paper.

For instance, if the number-one choice on one list matches the number-three choice on the other list, then that person would be the first name which matches. That person would be the person the couple should choose as their counselor.

The couple needs to decide that either one may go to him for counsel or advice any time a difficulty arises. Each must give the other permission to call that man of God. If the husband has a question about child-rearing or about the marriage, he has permission from his wife to see their counselor because she has given that permission in advance. If the wife has a question about child-rearing or about the marriage, she has permission from her husband to see their counselor because he has given that permission in advance.

If he happens to discover that she went to see their counselor, he won't feel embarrassed or frightened or worried or concerned because he has already given his permission for her to do so. Likewise, if she happens to find out that he went to see their counselor, she won't feel embarrassed or frightened or worried because she has already given her permission for him to do so.

Allow me to explain from my perspective as a preacher. For 22 years, I have traveled around the country to preach. During much of that time, I have been an administrator and a teacher at Hyles-Anderson College. At this writing, my wife and I have been married nearly 23 years. We have two children. I have written two books on marriage; my wife has written three books on marriage. In our Fundamental circles, we are somewhat known as marriage counselors. However, our marriage is just as vulnerable and susceptible to the same attacks of Satan and to the same fleshly urges or temptations to which everyone else is subject. The same Devil who fights you fights me. The same world which attacks your faith attacks my faith. I am flesh, and I am weak on some days just as my fellow men are weak on some days.

While Cindy and I were engaged, we both decided that should a problem ever arise in our future marriage, we would not be too proud to seek good advice and counsel. We did exactly that. In our particular case, we chose two individuals as our counselors.

Most definitely, I am not talking about just seeing a counselor when an emergency arises. My wife and I decided that if we asked questions and received good advice and counsel for the simple questions, we could eliminate the emergencies, and I believe I can honestly say we have.

Cindy and I do not want to spend our lives living from

crisis to crisis. However, should a crisis occur, we both have enough confidence in our counselors and in each other that we can seek advice to help reconcile a difference or to see us through a difficulty.

No person knows what the will of God holds or what life will bring. Perhaps heartache, the loss of a child, a crippling disease of a spouse, an egregious error or sin, or perhaps even marital unfaithfulness will shake the foundations of a marriage. No one is immune from the attacks of Satan, disease, sickness, death, or tragedy. Because of those uncertainties of life, I want to have wise men on whom I can lean in times of need. Cindy and I chose men we could trust—men with whom we knew we could share our confidences.

The following are suggestions of whom I strongly recommend **NOT** to choose as counselors:

• **A best friend.** Choosing a best friend may open the door to biased opinions. I also believe there is too much risk of taking sides.

• **A peer.** A wise couple would not choose a peer as a marriage counselor. A peer very well would find it difficult to counsel one his own age.

• **Someone who is distanced by many miles.** A couple should choose a counselor in the local area whom they can trust and see easily, especially in the early years of marriage and the early years of child-rearing.

At this point in our reading, a list has been made and compared, and a counselor has been chosen. I cannot begin to express how vital to a lasting marriage relationship this choice can be. Once the man of God has been chosen, he should be contacted by the couple. He should be told that he has been chosen as the main counselor and asked if he would be willing to be the marriage counselor through the ensuing years of marriage.

~&)

Checklist and Review

1. Having a ___ can help keep the ___ problems from becoming ___ problems.

2. List four ideal people to consider as counselors.

3. When a difficulty arises, the husband or the wife must give the other ___ to contact the man of God they have chosen as their counselor.

4. List the three groups of people who would not make the best counselors.

THREE

Unfulfilled Expectations

ONE OF THE most significant causes of disappointment and bickering in the early days of marriage is unfulfilled expectations. There is no way an engaged couple can plan a marriage together, perhaps perusing magazines that depict honeymoon hot spots to attend, checking out the wedding gowns and the tuxedos, or choosing flowers and announcements, without developing in their hearts expectations for what each believes marriage should be. I don't believe anyone enters into the marriage hoping it fails. I don't believe two people get married hoping to have a mediocre or a "B" marriage. Though a couple may not expect an "A+" marriage, I sincerely believe everyone would love to have an "A+" marriage. Therein lies the beginning of unfulfilled expectations. Regardless of where a couple's expectations are, every couple has them.

In Luke 15, Jesus tells a story about a father who had two sons. The younger son is often referred to as "the prodigal son." A day came in that boy's life when he wanted to leave home and live apart from his father's control. He went to his father and made the statement, *"Father, give me the portion of goods that falleth to me."* (Luke 15:12b) Evidently, the son was of age, and the goods were part of his inheritance from his father. The son was simply asking for what he felt was coming to him.

Likewise, in a marriage, there is nothing wrong in expecting certain rights and privileges to be enjoyed. A married man has the right to expect a faithful wife, and a married lady has the right to expect a faithful husband. A wife has a right to a husband who will care for her needs financially, physically, and materially. These expectations are proper expectations.

In the same respect, a husband may expect his wife to clean the house. He has the right to expect a clean house and an affectionate wife. These kinds of expectations are proper expectations.

However, depending on how high these expectations are and how inexperienced and immature a spouse may be, an opening may be created for a measure of disappointment. Why? Many a young husband marries and expects his wife, on a scale of one to ten, to be a "10" as a cook. However, perhaps she hasn't spent a considerable number of hours in the kitchen, and she turns out to be a "5." In far too many cases, the husband is a very disappointed man, and his disappointment can become a point of contention. In intense moments, he may use his disappointment in her culinary skills as leverage to hurt and to say unkind words to her.

On the other hand, perhaps the wife grew up in a home with a very strong father who had a good, secure job with a good, reliable income. Needless to say, that father could materially provide an above average standard of living for his family. Suppose that wife marries a young man who has a relatively new job and is still on the lower end of the wage scale. Perhaps he has not been on the job long enough to save much money. Even though she knows these facts, she still may marry him thinking that he is going to provide for her to the same degree of comfort as her father once provided for her. The new husband simply cannot meet those expectations.

The new wife expects, on a scale of one to ten, her new husband to be a "10" (like her father) with providing physical and material security. In reality, he may be barely a "4" at this time in his life. Of course, if the new wife is immature, she is likely to be very disappointed which can result in agitation and frustration. She may then resort to harsh words such as, "You're not a real man like my father; he took good care of me." Those kinds of statements contain biting, stinging, and demeaning words to a man. He may well feel that his manhood has been threatened; certainly, his pride has been injured.

Unfulfilled expectations can cause weakness in the marriage. If that weakness is not reconciled, it can be a life-long insult that gives way to bitterness. That bitterness festers like a cancer until eventually the foundation of the marriage is undermined. When the storms of life blow against it, that marriage crumbles because of a weakened foundation—all because of not reconciling unfulfilled expectations. In my many years of counseling, I have found that marriages seldom fail due to the big problems such as the death of a child or a life-threatening illness. Far too often, the little unresolved difficulties or unfulfilled expectations are what cause the downfall of a marriage. The difference between what a person expects and what he receives is the measure of a person's unhappiness or the measure of his joy.

> *"Far too often, the little unresolved difficulties or unfulfilled expectations are what cause the downfall of a marriage."*

On the other hand, if a young man enters a marriage with a young inexperienced wife and expects her to be about a "6" or a "7" as a cook, he will not be disappointed when he finds out that she is a "6." His acceptance of her abilities exactly as they are allows her room for growth to please him more, and it allows his measure of happiness to grow with her experience and ability.

If a young woman marries and expects her new husband to be about a "5" or a "6" as far as providing materially for her, she won't be disappointed when she discovers he is "5." Thus, she is fulfilled as a wife because she received what she expected. Her acceptance of her husband exactly as he is allows him to grow and mature in his ability to provide. Acceptance is so important.

Of course, in some areas such as faithfulness and behavior with the opposite gender, the expectation and the performance must always be a "10." Neither a husband nor a wife can be a "4" in faithfulness; they each must be a "10."

In combating the hurt of unfulfilled expectations, I am addressing maturity and experience. I'm addressing the youthfulness or inexperience (of one never before having been married) trying his best to provide for someone who has likewise never before been married. Therefore, I feel it is very important that I address just a few of the following areas of responsibility that need to be considered:

- the areas of cooking and cleaning
- the area of material provisions
- the kind of car being operated
- the quality or expense of the clothing worn
- the frequency of new clothing being purchased
- the purchasing of accessories for the wardrobe
- the kind of neighborhood in which the couple lives
- the areas of lawn care and landscaping

- the quality of furniture
- the acquiring of household appliances

A new husband might not be able to provide a washer and a dryer for his wife, though she had all of those helps and conveniences at home. In the beginning, a newly married couple may not be able to afford two cars or even one car. For the first months of marriage, they might have to buy an older, used car or even borrow someone else's car on occasion. Certainly, I would hope there is enough money saved to provide basic necessities.

These areas of expectations will be fulfilled as the spouse matures. In the beginning, the level of expectation should be low enough to accommodate the skill level each spouse has on the wedding day and not what each spouse will possess five or ten years from the wedding date.

Think of this whole idea of expectations in light of a toddler learning to walk and to run. A mother and father do not scold the young toddler when he falls over while taking his first few steps or when he cannot run without toppling. Sometimes parents record the first steps with video camera. Many take snapshots for memories. Those tottering steps bring smiles and enjoyment. Likewise, a new wife and a new husband should enjoy their early days of marriage—those early days of growing and learning.

When I first married Cindy, I found, to my delight, she was a good cook. However, she did not have a large variety of dishes she could prepare well. We ate many meals with chicken as the main dish. We also had a lot of meals with eggs as the main ingredient. For breakfast, we frequently had toast and hot cereals.

Now my wife has become a very accomplished cook, and she is confident with her cooking skills. As I think back to those early days (about the first six months we were married), my wife would usually make two meals each evening. She would experiment with one meal—trying to perfect it. Often that meal would wind up in the garbage can. Then, she would prepare a meal that she had proven and was confident in making and set that on the table.

After we had finished that meal, I would often make some excuse to leave the room. I would go to the garbage can, fish out the other meal, and finish that one off also! I enjoyed both meals, and I also understood that Cindy was not going to be an accomplished cook at 19 years of age when we married. I also understood that she was not going to be the cook that she would later become.

That illustration could fit nearly every aspect of the early days of marriage. With any kind of skill, each spouse must lower his expectation to where his spouse is. Let me reiterate again; I am certainly not referring to moral skills. I am not addressing faithfulness to church nor a spouse's walk with God. A couple's faithfulness to their marriage vows is not included. I believe that once a couple marries, they should be 100 percent faithful to each other. I believe they should be totally faithful while engaged and going steady. There is no room for error in those moral matters.

For example, when I was a very young and inexperienced preacher, I was traveling some and preaching and learning how to preach. Cindy's father was a superb preacher. She decided when we got married that she would not compare her inexperienced husband-preacher to her veteran preacher-dad. That gave me time and room to grow and mature in my preaching.

Let me return to the story of the prodigal son. As I said before, he made the statement, *"Father, give me the portion of goods that falleth unto me."* Though he was asking for that which was rightfully his, his character level was not able to handle what he received. In other words, though he had the right to what his father gave him, he was not prepared to deal with the responsibility. Later on, after he had made tragic mistakes and wasted what his father had given him, he came to the place in his life where he said, *"Father, I have sinned against heaven, and in thy sight, and am no more worthy to be called thy son."* (Luke 15:21b) In other words, he was saying, "Father, forgive me." The prodigal son went from saying, "Father, *give* me," to "Father, *forgive* me."

To be sure, there will be times in a marriage when mistakes will be made. There will be disagreements. Many disagreements are the result of unfulfilled expectations. Therefore, in the next chapter, I want to address how to handle disagreements.

ᕲ

Checklist and Review

1. A man should have his bills paid and enough money saved to provide a ___ and the equivalent of ___ months' rent or house payment.

2. A lady should learn ___ how to cook a variety of meals, how to plan a menu, and how to clean and organize the house.

3. If the new bride will be working, some of the chores and duties should be evenly ___ by both husband and wife.

4. When a spouse fails to meet the expectations of his marriage partner, great ___ is the usual result.

5. In many new marriages, the new husband and the

new wife often expect a performance of a ___ (on a scale of one to ten) from each other.

6. A new husband will probably not be able to attain a "10" with providing his new wife ___ and ___ security.

7. The weakening of a marriage is often brought about by ___.

8. The downfall of a marriage is usually caused NOT by failing to deal with the big problems of life but by failing to resolve the ___ difficulties.

9. The one definite area of marriage in which even newlyweds must score a "10" is that of ___.

FOUR

How to Handle Disagreements

L EARNING TO "FIGHT fair" in the marriage relationship is
crucial. Two human beings together in a lifelong, marital
relationship cannot expect to have 100 percent agreement all
the time in every area. If such a thing as clones existed, the
clones might be able to do that, but what a very boring relationship! Some of the very factors that attract two members
of the opposite gender are the differences that make them
unique persons.

For instance, as a rule, strong masculine men are drawn
to sweet feminine ladies. However, that sweet feminine
charm that was so intriguing will sometimes come out in a
very different attitude or perception or understanding of a
situation than the way the strong masculine mind might
think! Therefore, every couple must learn to handle disagreements in an agreeable way.

Disagreements will come—no doubt about it! Depending
on personality and how a person handles problems will
determine the reaction. Some people calmly handle situations. Some people react in what I call a slow burn on the
inside. Some people throw things, punch walls and slam
doors. Some feel the need to get away; they take a drive or a
walk around the block. Still others enjoy a good, old-fash-

ioned, knock-down, drag-out, verbal war. Certainly, I have my own feelings about how a couple should handle disagreements. I want to list 15 statements about "fighting fair" in marriage. I learned many of these principles from my father and my father-in-law, probably the best marriage warriors I know.

In I Peter 3:7, a husband is admonished to dwell with his wife according to knowledge. "Likewise, ye husbands, dwell with them according to knowledge, giving honour unto the wife, as unto the weaker vessel, and as being heirs together of the grace of life; that your prayers be not hindered." A husband is supposed to know his wife, and, in the same respect, a wife should know her husband. A husband should know his wife well enough to expect her automatic reaction or response to a crisis or problem. Likewise, a wife should know her husband well enough to expect his automatic reaction to a crisis or problem.

I have watched my mother and my father build one of the best marriages I have ever seen. That is not to say that my parents' marriage is one where there have never been any disagreements. Yes, my mother and father disagreed at times, but they handled their disagreements wisely. Through the years, my wife and I have learned to utilize the same methods my parents used to build their marriage.

1. Get on the same side of the fence. Some people like to argue just for the sake of arguing. However, I don't believe that method is the best way to build a strong marriage. I believe couples should seek to want to be on the same side, though I don't mean the husband and the wife have to view the situation in the same way.

Let me illustrate. In World War II, the United States had many allies who were close and dear friends of our nation, such as the British. We had allies who were in desperate need of our aid, like the French. We also had allies who could have been considered an enemy, such as Russia. These allies, with their differing political ideology, decided we had to fight on the same side in this particular war. That alliance did not mean that those in power had to see the war through the same eyes but that they had to fight on the same side.

Allow me to liken the allies of World War II to partners in a marriage. Just as the Allies joined together against a common foe, it is so important for a husband and wife to become allies with one another—not enemies. Far too easily a certain matter of contention can outweigh the importance of the marriage. Then the marriage will suffer at the expense of proving that one is right.

When a disagreement comes, the couple must affirm their friendship and alliance to one another. When a disappointment or a disagreement arises but before the knock-down, drag-out, verbal battle erupts, the couple should say to one another, "You are my friend; you are my companion, and I love you. I don't happen to see the situation your way, but I am on your side. I'm on your team."

The quarterback on a football team may disagree with a certain play the coach sends in to him. Still, in order to have a successful game, both have to see the game plan the same way. Even as the quarterback executes a certain play or passes the football, he may think in his heart, "We should have had a different play for this down." Still, even if he disagrees vehemently, he has to be on the same team with that coach.

Just as a coach and his quarterback will occasionally disagree, at some time or another, a couple will disagree with each other. Always remember when the disagreement comes, the couple must affirm to each other that they are on the same team. That affirmation doesn't mean there won't be disagreements; it merely means that the couple is placing themselves on the same side of the fence.

2. Agree readily with your adversary. *"Agree with thine adversary quickly, whiles thou art in the way with him...."* (Matthew 5:25a) To observe this principle takes some greatness. If a married couple does not see eyeball to eyeball, one of the quickest ways to diffuse a potentially sensitive problem is for one person to say, "I agree with you," or "You have a good point," or "Hmm, that is interesting; I didn't see the situation that way," or "Wow! I wish I had seen it that way before," or "I'm glad you showed me that angle." The person is not saying that his spouse is right; he is simply agreeing that his spouse has a right to a different opinion.

In September of 1993, Israeli prime minister, Yitzhak Rabin, and the Palestine Liberation Organization chairman, Yasser Arafat, agreed to the signing of a historic peace accord. After witnessing the signing, the longtime foes shook hands in the presence of the United States President, Bill Clinton. I often say to married couples, what a shame it is that these warring nations with centuries of hate and murder could come to terms of peace and unity, while a husband and wife with love for each other cannot come to terms of peace!

On the other hand, a married couple who love each other and has promised vows of allegiance to each other get into arguments where they won't speak with each other for days and weeks. I submit that if warring nations can sit down to talk at their peace table, a married couple ought to be able to sit down and talk at their peace table.

The first step to doing that is for the couple to affirm they are on the same team, and the second step is for each spouse to give each other the right to his own opinion. A husband may think that his opinion is the only correct one, but his spouse may also think her opinion is correct; therefore, each must give the other the proper respect of a human being.

Even casual acquaintances would give one another the proper respect of saying, "You are entitled to your opinion." Every person deserves the gift of human dignity and a right to a personal opinion.

A married couple should say sincerely to each other, "I respect your right to disagree with me. I respect your right to have your own thoughts, and I want to know and hear your thoughts. I want to see if perhaps I should see it from a different angle than I now see it."

3. Decide whether or not to win an argument or build a relationship. If the only interest is in winning an argument, the marriage is going to suffer. On the other hand, a couple can use the friction to further strengthen and encourage their relationship. The result is totally up to the couple.

In my mind, I haven't yet been in an argument that is worth my marriage. Whether the argument concerns money, a car, damage to a vehicle, an accident, different driving styles, a meal, cooking, housecleaning, my job, or my office, I have yet to find a situation that is worth arguing about at the expense of my marriage. I want to build the marriage relationship Cindy and I enjoy.

When disagreeing, one spouse should take the initiative and say, "We disagree, and we don't see eyeball to eyeball on this situation, but I want you to know that wherever we wind up in this decision, I want our marriage to be stronger. I want us to be building a relationship—not simply trying to win an argument."

4. Sleep on the situation. What good advice my dad gave me when he taught me this principle! He said, "Jack, no matter how difficult the situation, many times a good night's rest will give both of you a new perspective about the situation. Your mind can go to work on it."

It is amazing how much clearer a couple can see things on a matter in the morning. The thinking process is clearer in the morning. Anger can be diffused by a good night's rest. Sometimes a couple may need to sleep on the decision longer than one evening. If a situation arises where the couple cannot see eye to eye on an important issue and if the marriage seems to be drifting apart, one person needs to suggest, "Let's take some time to not discuss the issue. Let's go on with the rest of our marriage. Let's give our minds, our hearts, our spirits, and our prayer time to this situation. Let's give God time to help us come together on this matter." Focus on the other avenues of life and decide on a time when the matter will once again be discussed.

Suppose a husband comes home from work on a Tuesday night and finds his wife has something on her heart and mind—something that has bothered her all day. Perhaps the children have been misbehaving, and, at the same time, the husband's work day did not go well. When he arrives home, both are in a bad mood, and both get into a verbal scuffle, an argument, if you please.

One gives the infamous silent treatment causing the other to get more upset. Words are exchanged, provoking and escalating the verbal battle into a louder volume with more intensity. Deciding to talk it out and thrashing it back and forth often doesn't bring the needed answers. What the heated argument does bring is hurt mirrored in faces and voices.

At that point, the wise spouse will say something like this, "It is obvious we don't agree. It is obvious that neither one of us is able to come to a solution right now. I really believe that this issue is an important matter, but I really believe that I am in no shape to fix the situation right now. I am not strong enough emotionally, mentally, or spiritually right now to try to fix this problem. Let's sleep on it, and talk about it on Friday night. I promise that we will get into it as deeply as we both can. I promise that we will come to a conclusion. Let's take a little time to rest our minds and bodies and see it through different eyes a couple days from now."

5. Don't discuss controversial matters late at night. In my book, *Dating with a Purpose,* I wrote that what dating couples would not consider doing immorally at 7:00 p.m., they could very possibly be engaging in at 11:30 p.m. or later. As the evening progresses, defenses wear down, and couples become more vulnerable—especially to bad news or to critical spirits. Therefore, I encourage married couples not to discuss controversial matters late at night.

My wife and I have an agreement that we will not discuss major (or even minor) matters differences after 8:00 p.m. Ending any day on a sour note is absolutely senseless.

6. I recommend that a couple should not bring up disagreeable matters when first getting together. For example, after just waking up would be an inappropriate time to have a discussion—especially a discussion that could have some negatives. The first few minutes after the husband arrives home in the evening would also be a very poor time to discuss negative matters.

That first meeting is so important and vital. When the husband comes home from work, he and his wife should eat supper, enjoy the meal together, and after the dishes are finished, take a walk around the block. Then they can bring up the matter needing attention. If children are in the home, then when they are playing after the meal, the parents could sit down in the living room to discuss the matter away from the children. A couple should bring up issues to discuss when their minds are more relaxed and their time together is not hurried or open to interruptions.

7. One spouse should take up the argument for his partner. If a couple really love each other, they can handle disagreements almost like a game. Any couple can make it a game of love, wherein one person loves another so much that he takes up the argument for his loved one and tries to win.

My dad was a master at this "game." He would actually take my mother's side on an issue and argue it *for* her *against* himself. It is quite difficult to get upset or angry with a husband who takes up the club his wife was going to use to hit him and hits himself with it! Almost immediately, my mother would jump to Dad's defense and take his side. Thus, they were united quickly on the issue.

8. Redirect the anger to another unrelated issue. This is a delicate concept, but one that I have watched my dad successfully employ many times. For instance, perhaps a wife is upset or angry about the way a person treated a child or even the way her husband was treated on the job. Often without thinking, she vents her anger or frustration toward her husband. Perhaps a wife is upset at the way her husband has or has not cared for a household responsibility. Invariably, he feels the heat of her anger. Often, that anger can be redirected to a different issue.

In marriage counseling, I will sometimes instruct a wife to criticize me or to blame me for a marital problem. Let me further explain that there are a number of ladies who come alone to our Sunday services. For one reason or another, their husbands do not attend our services. Such a husband sometimes become jealous of his wife's pastor or of a Sunday school teacher. Without provocation, a husband sometimes starts thinking that his wife is a touch more infatuated with the church than she is with him.

Therefore, we counselors will recommend to that wife to seemingly criticize the pastor by making a statement such as:

"I thought that pastor would never get done preaching. He preached forever today." Even though she might not feel that deeply, making such a statement diffuses the hurt, the anger, or the resentment her husband has. Sometimes we have been able to win that husband to our church and to ourselves because the wife wisely directed her husband's anger to a third, unrelated issue.

It takes wisdom and finesse to redirect anger and hurt feelings. A couple cannot let anger come between them. It is far better to get angry at someone unseen or unknown to diffuse the anger rather than to let anger fester.

I have found much of our frustration arises from situations that we cannot fix. Perhaps something is wrong with the house. A wife often blames her husband when he might not have the ability or the aptitude to fix the problem. The husband could diffuse the situation by simply and wisely saying, "I agree with you. I'm frustrated with this house, too. Sometimes I want to kick in a door or sell the place. Sometimes I get angry and frustrated about the builder who obviously didn't know what he was doing. I wish I had known he didn't know one thing about building. He should have his business license revoked." It is better for a couple to get aggravated at somebody they don't see or don't even know and to diffuse the anger than to let that anger fester at one another.

Oftentimes, when a wife realizes that her husband is just as frustrated as she is, it makes her feel that she's not all alone in her disappointment. So often, people take general statements as personal attacks against their character when actually they are just hearing simple frustrations being vented, though not very wisely expressed. For instance, a husband might be frustrated with a meal, when his real frustration is with the fact that his job didn't go well that day. He picks at his food, and his wife thinks he is upset about her meal. She says, "Don't you like the meal?" So he criticizes: "Well, I never did like chicken anyway. You make the same chicken all the time, and I hate corn. You know I hate corn."

The wise wife will read between the lines and realize he is saying unkind words (though he shouldn't) because something else is involved. Instead of becoming frustrated with his behavior and words, she could say: "I tried to make tasty chicken, but it is just impossible with that old oven." Or she could say, "I'm getting so disgusted with the meat department. I try to buy meat, and it has far too much fat on it. That guy down there at the meat market should be fired for hiding the fat under the meat. He is just hiking the price."

The wise husband will realize that his wife is entering into his frustration with him. She is diffusing his anger. Before they know it, the couple won't be disgusted with the meat department or the oven. The real truth will come out, and the husband might be able to share with his wife his true frustrations and feelings. She can then become a companion, a friend, and a counselor as she realizes his anger was not with the meal, but with anger and frustration in general. Performing this fine art takes some wisdom. It takes being a good Christian and a confident spouse. Redirecting anger takes a spouse who will look beyond the words and see the heart of the person he loves.

9. The wise person will allow a spouse to react. Then he should ask himself, "Is it the problem that is upsetting me or is it the reaction to the problem?" If a person could somehow divorce the words from the real issue, he could fix the problem very quickly. Many times, I can listen to a couple fuss in my office and immediately see the problem and the solution. Within minutes, we often have the problem fixed, thereby ending the need for argument. If either the husband or the wife had allowed for a reaction, they would have eliminated the argument and would not have needed to seek counsel. A married couple must try to separate the reaction of a spouse from the problem at hand.

10. **The wise wife will understand that the man wants to solve the problem.** A wife usually wants her husband to feel the same way as she does. This just happens to be a basic difference between a male and female. Usually a man will quickly say, "Let's fix this problem." However, a wife wants her husband to feel like she does before he fixes the problem. A woman wants a companion to feel the same degree of emotion that she feels, and a man simply wants to eliminate controversy.

I teach a man to take time to let his wife get everything out of her system. He should let her say what is on her heart, and when she is all done saying it, he shouldn't answer, "Oh, that is nothing; I can fix that."

While she is revealing her heart, he can be responding with statements like, "Huh, is that right? Wow! Well, I'll be. Oh, yes." He should be giving his wife voice inflection and eye contact that says, "I care." The wise husband will look her right in the eye, groan a little bit like he is with her, and agree with her.

He should hear her out, take her hand, and say, "Tell me more about it. I want to hear everything you feel about it. When she is all talked out, he should then say, "I'm so glad you told me about that. You know while you were talking to me, I had this idea. I believe I know a way to fix it. Let me tell you what I think about it." The wise husband will tell his wife what he is thinking, and then fix the situation. Every wife needs someone who wants to hear and feel and see her heart, and, at the same time, that wife needs a fixer of the problems as well.

11. Don't believe any words spoken in anger.
Perhaps a wife will make a statement like, "You always are so clumsy." "You never say, 'I love you.'" "You never fix anything around here." "You are always getting in the way." I submit to every married couple that the use of *always* and *never* should be avoided. Often those statements cause angry retaliation. The husband might retort, "I hate the way you do that." "I can't stand it when you're just like your mother."

The wise spouse understands when strong words are used in anger that those words aren't always accurate. Vehemence is usually the voice of insecurity trying to reinforce itself. Strong, angry words are used by a scared person who is trying to capture another's attention. Those words can often be interpreted as "I'm scared!" "I'm angry!" "I feel insecure, and I need strength right now!" Angry words and accusations usually evolve out of a situation where one person feels unfairly treated, so he uses strong language which causes a more uncontrolled situation. Instead of throwing water on the "fire," gasoline is thrown. Let me ask a question. In dealing with the people you love, are you a bucket of water on the fire of anger, or are you a bucket of gasoline? Are you a fireman, or are you an arsonist?

12. Decide on some absolutes by which to abide.
For instance, in our home, Cindy and I never use the word *divorce*. I happen to believe no married couple should ever use the word in anger or in jest. I believe to use the word *divorce* is to be open to an idea that could lead to divorce. Another absolute to consider is never to argue about the intimate marital relationship. I believe that bringing the bedroom participation into the arena of argument is to create a wound so deep and painful that bitterness is the only natural result. The marriage will be damaged in a far, far greater way than in any other way it could be hurt. The act of physical love is

sacred. Hebrews 13:4a says, *"Marriage is honourable in all, and the bed undefiled...."*

A couple who is experiencing intimacy problems should go straight to the marriage counselor and allow him to wisely and carefully counsel the situation. Most assuredly a couple should never argue about bedroom relationships nor use the word divorce.

Keep in mind that couples may have skirmishes, but even those must be fought fairly. In 1864, an international agreement was signed called the Geneva Convention. This agreement established a code for the wartime care and treatment of the sick, wounded, and dead as well as prisoners of war, including the protection of hospitals, etc. having the emblem of the Red Cross. With the development of far more devastating weaponry such as nerve gas, the Geneva Convention was later revised. Countries such as the United States, Great Britain, and France abided by the Geneva Convention. On the other hand, some countries had no regard for the Geneva Convention. Many of those countries lost their wars and suffered severe reprisals because of the way in which they fought the war. Even wars must be fought by certain rules. Even a marriage has to have a "Geneva Convention."

Every couple should have some absolutes, some areas that won't be discussed. The following are some absolutes in our family:

- I do not criticize my wife's family.
- My wife does not criticize my family.
- We do not fight in front of the children. Parents should not let their children hear angry, harsh words. A couple should have the discipline to care for a difficulty while alone and away from the children.

13. Enjoy making up. Undoubtedly, making up has to be the best part of having an argument! Reconciling is one reason why a couple should not use sexual language or sexual behavior in arguments. The intimate marital relationship is a wonderful place to run to as the couple reconciles, re-establishes, and strengthens their marriage after it has been wounded by some harsh words. A married couple should enjoy making up. When a couple makes up, they should give themselves to each other. The battlefield should be kept outside of the bedroom.

14. The married couple must realize they are in the marriage for the long haul. A short-term squabble may last a week, or even a month. Usually, it lasts a couple of days or a few hours at most. What is that amount of time compared to 50 or 60 years of marriage? A couple marries for the long haul; therefore, they need to be patient with each other. If one spouse has seemingly brought about a major calamity in the marriage and caused disappointment, the other should remain patient. No temporary crisis should permanently disable a marriage.

A person may battle cancer and undergo chemotherapy treatments for a year. Even though his life is miserable, he will bounce back. In many cases, the rest of that person's life will be healthy, strong, and good. The person may enjoy many years of wonderful living.

In the same way as a person physically suffers the effects of cancer, a marriage might be afflicted with a verbal "cancer." The couple may survive a bad year in marriage. I contend the next 20 years should not be wasted because of one bad year. When a couple marries for the long haul, they must learn to be patient with each other.

15. A couple must discuss the difficulty. The couple should plunge in and talk through the problem. They must not harbor bad feelings which will fester like a cancer. The name of the game is communication. A married couple has to talk out the difficulty, just as warring nations eventually come to the peace table and negotiate.

A diplomat might say some hot words, or he might even say the wrong thing. However, wars are stopped when leaders learn to discuss the situation. Talk is not cheap; talk is golden. Someone said that silence is golden, but sometimes it is just plain "yellow"!

A couple must learn to talk with each other. In counseling people involved in an extramarital affair, I have discovered in almost every case that one of the two guilty persons said, "We could talk." Sometimes the man ran off with what I would call a rather unattractive woman. In most cases, the other woman wasn't nearly as attractive as his wife, but he could talk with her. That is just one of the reasons why couples must learn to discuss their difficulties.

Marriage is a mirror. Your partner reflects through his or her reactions your strengths or weaknesses. To put it another way, the weaknesses of your partner provide you the opportunity to show your strengths or to explore your own weaknesses. Please don't run from this wonderful opportunity; instead, work on your weaknesses and learn to be strong for each other. Every relationship needs to be worked on regularly.

I trust this chapter will profit every couple who reads it in years to come. All I desire for every marriage is happiness. I want every couple to build their marriage. I want every couple to pass on to their children the value and virtue of marriage. I also especially desire that children can look at their parents and say, "I want a marriage just like the one Mom and Dad have." Let's make that our goal!

❧

Checklist and Review

1. It is crucial in the marriage relationship for the couple to learn to ___.

2. Every newlywed needs to be aware of the fact that ___ will come—no doubt about it!

3. Though couples do not need to view every situation in exactly the same way, they should still seek to be on the ___.

4. Every married couple should have a ___ at which to sit, talk, and solve problems.

5. To come to amiable terms with each other, a couple needs to agree in two areas:
   a. They need to ___ they are on the same team.
   b. They need to give each other the ___ to have differing opinions.

6. Because the thinking process is always sharper in the morning, a good night's rest can nearly always defuse ___.

7. Some of the most inaccurate of words and thoughts are those spoken in ___.

8. The best part about having a disagreement is ___.

FIVE

The In-Law Relationship

THE WISE COUPLE will develop a personal and unique relationship (apart from each other) with every member of their respective families. I believe the husband should get to know his wife's dad, her mother, and her siblings. I further believe he should have a special relationship with his wife's dad and mother apart from her.

If his father-in-law enjoys a certain hobby or sport, the wise husband will learn that hobby or sport and join with him. If the father-in-law has a unique interest, the wise husband will learn that interest. I believe it is very important for the father-in-law and the son-in-law to build a relationship unique to them and apart from their wives.

Likewise, I believe the husband should get to know his wife's mother. Certainly, that relationship would be more limited, but I believe the wise husband could and should write an occasional note to her or have an occasional chat on the phone.

In the 23 years that Cindy and I have been married, Mrs. Hyles and I have chatted on the phone many times. My wife and my father chat about life and about the children and family often on the phone. When my dad and Cindy are talking, I do not talk on the phone with them. I am happy that my father and my wife have a relationship that is somewhat apart from me.

The wise couple will want to build relationships with the other family members apart from each other.

1. The wise husband will care for the material well-being of his wife. Her family will judge not by how much prayer or how much Bible reading he does. They will not judge him by how great a soul winner he is. They will judge by how well their daughter (or their sister) is treated. Certainly, a new husband won't be able to buy his wife her own car right away or put her up in a mansion, but he can take good care of her. When he gets a little extra money, he should buy her a new dress or take her out to eat. When a husband shows his wife little considerations, word will get back to her parents that he is taking good care of their daughter.

2. The wise wife will learn to clean house and cook well. In my marriage counseling sessions, I have found that the husband's mother can be a great ally or a great point of contention. After all, she has taken care of her little boy for many years. She has cleaned for him and cooked for him; in her mind, no one will do as good of a job as she has been able to do. (She might be right!) The new wife is not as experienced as his mother is. However, a new wife can begin concentrating on some skills now. She can develop her cooking and cleaning abilities.

I often recommend that a wife-to-be find some good cooks in her church and spend time with them. She can make appointments to be with them. In First Baptist Church, a lady named Louise Clifton was probably the very best cook I ever met in my life. She is in Heaven now, and I miss her sorely. I often joke and say, "If Louise Clifton is not cooking in Heaven, I'm not sure if I want to go there!"

When my wife was a little girl, Mrs. Clifton was her baby-sitter. During Cindy's teenage years, she and Mrs. Clifton remained good buddies and pals. Before Cindy and I were married, and then for the first several years after we were married, Cindy made regular appointments to go to Mrs. Clifton's house to learn how to can and freeze vegetables. Mrs. Clifton taught Cindy how to prepare strawberry preserves, how to make muffins, how to make gravy, how to prepare a fancy meal and how to plan for a house full of company. My wife profited greatly from the experience and wisdom of Louise Clifton. Every wife-to-be needs to find somebody like Mrs. Clifton in her church. She should seek that lady's help and learn everything she can from her.

For a wedding gift, Mrs. Clifton gave us a recipe box full of her recipes. As I mentioned elsewhere, Cindy practiced making those recipes and has become a very proficient, excellent cook. I owe much to the wise, helpful, and loving training of Mrs. Clifton.

Ladies should also learn to clean the house well. I realize cleaning should be natural; unfortunately, it is not. There is a science to cleaning a house. If a wife doesn't know how to clean, her husband might well come home and criticize. He shouldn't, but more than likely, he will. A new wife might hear, "Let me show you how my mother did this." (A husband should never say such words.) However, I must say that a wife should never give her husband a reason to say unkind words because of her inability to clean the house.

The wife who is not proficient in the area of cleaning should go to someone who is an excellent cleaner and learn how she cleans each room of the house. The ideal situation is for the mother to teach the daughters, but in this day, many mothers fail in teaching and training their daughters. How sad for mothers to fail in following the admonition given in Titus 2:3-5, *"The aged women likewise, that they be in behaviour as becometh holiness, not false accusers, not given to much wine, **teachers of good things; That they may teach the young women** to be sober, to love their husbands, to love their children, To be discreet, chaste, keepers at home, good, obedient to their own husbands, that the word of God be not blasphemed."* A wife should never be so proud as to think that she knows how to do it all.

3. The wise couple will push each other toward their immediate family. The wise husband will encourage his wife to spend time with her family. Even though the husband is still in the picture, he will encourage his wife to love her dad and to remain her daddy's little girl. He should want her to remain good buddies with her mom and dad. The wise husband will not want to drive a wedge between his wife and her family.

Statistics say that 85 percent of what makes up a person is directly attributed to his parents. If a husband doesn't like his wife's parents, in essence, he is saying that he disapproves of 85 percent of what she is. I will acknowledge that some parents may have some bad habits. Perhaps they are not as good Christians as they ought to be. They might not be faithful in church. They might even smoke or drink. The wise couple will be careful about spending too much time with non-separated parents. When children come, no doubt the couple will be concerned with the influence the grandparents may have with the grandchildren. I must say this in their defense: They did rear a daughter who was worthy of marrying.

In the same respect, a wife should recognize that her husband owes a great deal of what he is to what his mother and father are. The wise wife will encourage her husband to spend time with his parents. By all means, I believe the wife should be present too, but she should allow her husband to see his dad and to spend private time with him.

My wife often says to me, "Jack, I like it when you enjoy being with your dad. You and your dad get along so well, and I really like it that you do." I feel as though my wife encourages me to spend time with my dad. Those kinds of statements from my wife affords me the freedom to invite her along or to encourage her to be with her family. I am not advocating husbands and wives spending great lengths of time away from each other. In fact, I believe extended separations are not wise.

In public, when my father-in-law, Brother Hyles, was introducing me to preach or to pray in our public services, he often said, "Jack Schaap is the finest son-in-law in all the world." Whether or not that statement is true, it was still a good statement for his daughter to hear. Then he often added, "Jack Schaap has encouraged his wife to be close to her dad and to her mom." He has also said on occasion that he is not threatened by me. I love the fact that Cindy is close to her mom and dad because that makes her happier. That close relationship also makes her feel more secure.

Certainly there are in-laws who can be meddling and troublesome. I advise every couple in that kind of situation to go straight to their marriage counselor for advice on how to handle that particular situation.

4. The wise couple will never, never, never criticize their in-laws. A wise husband will defend his in-laws or shut up, but he will never criticize them. In the same respect, a wise wife will defend her husband's parents and never criticize them.

5. The wise couple will plan a schedule of when to visit in-laws. The couple will plan in advance what to do for the holidays—where to stay and how long to stay. Sometimes the in-laws feel threatened because they have no assurance that the newlyweds want to be with them.

When my wife and I married, my parents, who live about two and one-half hours away from us, were a little worried that I would not be home at all. They thought they were only going to see me on rare occasions. So Cindy and I together planned a schedule and then sought advice from our marriage counselor. We planned a monthly visit to my parents, and they were ecstatic because they thought they were only going to see me once or twice a year. They did not know they were going to see me 12 times a year, plus some holidays.

In advance, Cindy and I planned the date, the time we would meet, and how much money we could spend. We planned these times to be like little mini-vacations. My parents were close enough that we could drive to and from their home in one day. Those visits made my parents feel secure that our marriage was not causing them to forfeit a son. In actuality, they even saw me a little more than they had before I was married.

6. The wise couple will plan what role the in-laws will have with the children—their grandchildren. If the in-laws are nearby and could, on occasion, provide baby-sitting services, they will need to be allowed more involvement. Perhaps the in-laws live a considerable distance away, and when they come to visit, they come for one or two weeks. In order to enjoy the other 49 weeks of absence from them, the married couple may have to accept some lengthier visits.

The wise couple will decide what role their parents will play in child rearing. I believe it is vital that the grandchildren see their grandparents. The intricate and complex problems a couple might have with their in-laws should not be a weapon used to hurt the sweet relationship of grandparent and grandchild. The wise couple will expect the grandparents to spoil their children. If the couple disciplines their children as they should 49 or 50 weeks out of the year, the grandparents are not going to ruin 50 weeks of training with two weeks of visiting! Some new attitudes may develop which need to be corrected when Grandma and Grandpa go home. If that becomes a problem, the couple should have a frank talk with the grandparents. The wise couple will explain in advance what type of behavior is acceptable. The children belong to the parents, not to the grandparents; therefore, the parents must be firm and fair in their discipline. At the same time, the parents should allow the grandparents to have a good relationship with their grandchildren.

Many grandparents are great baby-sitters, and they enjoy the privilege. If a couple allows that relationship, then they have to realize that their parents may visit unexpectedly. If a constant problem arises with grandparents visiting without advance notice, the husband should have a pleasant chat with his father-in-law. He should be honest and carefully explain that they are wanted and that their visits are enjoyed, but the visits must be by schedule rather than impromptu. Many times having a frank talk like this can be averted if, while planning the wedding and marriage, the couple will let their respective parents know even then that they will be included, that they will be invited to be a part of their new life together, and that they will not be excluded. Most problems arise from insecure people trying to force themselves into a relationship from which they feel they have been excommunicated. The wise couple will plan a way to see their in-laws; in so doing, rarely will problems arise between them.

If problems do arise, the wise couple will go to their marriage counselor for advice. If at some point intruding in-laws become a habitual problem, the husband will have to put his foot down and perhaps say, "We will visit each other at scheduled times, but you cannot get involved in my marriage." If it happens to be a worse case scenario, the wife may need to say to her parents, "Mom and Dad, I love you both with all of my heart, but you cannot meddle with my marriage." A husband may have to go to his mother and say, "Mom, I love you. You are the best mother in all the world, but you can't ever criticize my wife."

Once again, there are some absolutes to observe.

- A husband must not allow his parents to criticize his wife.
- A wife must not allow her parents to criticize her husband. My wife would never allow me to be criticized by her parents. To my knowledge, her parents never have criticized me. Again, she would never put up with it.

Invite your in-laws to have a part in your lives without running your lives. If they feel they must give their input on child rearing, firmly and frankly say something like this: "You had an opportunity to rear us, and your job is finished. Now it is our opportunity to rear our children. I was not there to give you input when you reared me, so please do not offer your input unless I ask you."

So much heartache can be bypassed if the couple will go to their parents and ask advice. What is wrong with asking, "I have a question about how you reared the children. We think thus and so. Do you have any input?" Sometimes a question like that opens the door to wonderful, helpful input. A couple can choose whether or not to obey the advice. Just being consulted often makes parents feel important and still a part of the lives of their married children.

7. **The wise couple will decide that their marriage will be made up of two members, not six or more.** Marriage should not consist of four in-laws telling two peo-

ple how to live. A couple has to live their marriage the way they believe God would have them do so, without interference from both sets of in-laws. The Bible very clearly states that when a husband marries, he is supposed to leave his father and mother, cleave to his wife and they shall be one flesh. *"For this cause* (marriage) *shall a man leave his father and mother, and cleave to his wife; And they twain shall be one flesh: so then they are no more twain, but one flesh. What therefore God hath joined together, let not man put asunder."* (Mark 10:7–9) A couple must build their marriage and plan how to accomplish that building process. In that plan, the wise couple will make a comfortable niche in their lives for parents.

8. The wise husband will brag on his spouse to his or her parents and vice versa. When the husband is with his wife's mom and dad, he should mention something specific that he likes about their daughter. He should let them think that they have done a good job of preparing her to be a wife. Likewise, when the wife is with her husband's parents, she should tell them something specific that she really likes about their son. She should want them to enjoy the pride of believing that they did a good job preparing their son for her. The wise husband should be very careful about bragging on his wife to his own mother. Most mothers would feel threatened by such comments, and, in the same respect, the wife should refrain from bragging about her husband to her father. He could feel threatened by that praise. Go easy on the bragging, but be sure to brag on him to his parents and brag on her to her parents.

∾

By employing these simple suggestions, harmony can be maintained in the home.

ᕦᑋᒶ

Checklist and Review

1. The father of the bride does not judge his son-in-law by his soul-winning ability or by how many chapters he reads in his Bible; rather, the father-in-law judges his son-in-law by how well his son-in-law ___ his daughter.

2. A wise husband will push his wife toward ___; likewise, a wise wife will push her husband toward ___.

3. Statistics show that 85% of what "makes" a person is directly attributed to that person's ___.

4. Wisdom dictates that a spouse ___ his/her in-laws and never ___ them.

5. Advance planning is required for a couple to work out the details of keeping the family happy, especially during the ___.

6. In-laws play a crucial role in the lives of their grandchildren; therefore, the wise couple will decide in advance what that ___ will be.

7. Four in-laws instructing two people how to live is not ___; the two people must live their marriage the way they believe ___ would have them.

SIX

Financial Bliss

Iᶠ I ʜᴀᴅ to choose one subject that produces more strife in the marriage and brings more people into the counseling office for marital help, I would have to choose the subject of finances. Who handles the money and how it is handled can become a very sensitive subject between a husband and a wife. Allow me to address some basic financial principles I believe a young couple should consider when setting up their finances for the first couple of years in the marriage.

The basic idea on which I operate is to set up finances so that it rarely, if ever, must be discussed. Personally, I believe the less a couple has to discuss sensitive or controversial issues, the more likely their marriage will be happy, and the less likely strife and controversy will occur. I do believe a young couple should discuss everything, and all married couples should learn to communicate freely. However, I have found when a subject like finances must be discussed, it is usually during an emergency or crisis time or when the husband or wife feels like his material needs are being neglected. Let me share several basic and practical statements about this sensitive subject of finances.

1. Decide who will be responsible for the family credit reputation. If a couple is unable to decide, I usually recommend that the husband be the responsible person for several reasons. First, the woman has taken his last name—the name both will bear for the rest of their married life together. That is not the most important criteria, but usually a man is sensitive about his credit record and his name. *"A good name is rather to be chosen than great riches, and loving favour rather than silver and gold."* (Proverbs 22:1)

However, sometimes the wife is unusually good with numbers, with caring for a budget, with making the practical decisions of paying monthly bills and with deciding how to distribute money. Whoever is the responsible person is not the issue; one person needs to be in charge of the family credit reputation. Consider the truth of the old phrase, "If everybody is in charge, then nobody is in charge." Two heads cannot run a marriage. One person has to have the final say-so of what should or should not be done regarding the matter of money.

2. Give the person in charge the right and power to guard that family credit reputation. Usually, when I am counseling with a young couple, I almost immediately discover that both know who should be in charge of the finances. Right away, the husband will look to his wife and say, "She is the best one with the money," or vice versa. When a decision is made and one person is chosen to head the finances, the other needs to give the one in charge the authority and the right to be the financial manager in that marriage. When a crisis or controversy comes, the person in charge then has the authority and permission from his spouse to make the tough decisions.

3. A couple should define what rules to live by in order to protect their good financial name. A couple should follow some basic guidelines. The Biblical order that God has set forth is to first earn the money, save it, and then pay for the desired purchases. There may be some incurment of debt in a new marriage. I am personally not opposed to going into debt for justifiable liabilities such as a house or perhaps a car. I do believe it is unwise to go into debt for products or items that are quickly consumed, such as food, clothing, or entertainment.

Many in our generation have developed the "enjoy-now-pay-later" mentality which is so dangerous. A couple should earn the right to have those big, expensive items. I don't believe that it is wrong to go into debt when purchasing a house if the house is in the right neighborhood and wisely chosen. Actually, the purchase of a house can be looked at as an asset that will increase in value. However, the average house appreciates at a rate of three to five percent per year while the average mortgage loan rate can be six to nine percent per year. Unless you pay off your mortgage at a fast rate, you will be losing money. Of course, renting is an option, but 100% of your rent money is lost when compared to the 6 to 9% you lost when purchasing a house. Likewise, an automobile can be used as transportation back and forth from work. That vehicle is a valuable tool in developing and building the financial assets.

SOME RULES FOR MONEY MANAGEMENT

Checking Accounts

I believe that both the husband and the wife should have their own independent checking accounts and perhaps their own independent savings accounts. Advocating separate checking accounts does not mean that I am trying to divide the home. I am merely trying to let both the husband and the wife each have a measure of independence and a measure of security which allows each a little bit of freedom to choose how to spend his allocation of money.

If a wife has to come to her husband every time she needs new hosiery or a new cooking utensil or because she would like to try some new perfume, the husband could feel harassed. This situation could get to the point where he feels like he is the father having to provide for his child. Likewise, if the wife is in charge, it would be easy for the husband to feel put down or have his masculine ego bruised when his wife says he cannot have $10 to purchase some golf balls. The result is one spouse feeling that he is almost in bondage to the person in charge of the money.

Therefore, I recommend that whoever is in charge of the money should set aside a portion of money to be allocated to the spouse who is not in charge. That allowance should be given for discretionary use. For that reason, I believe there should be two separate checkbooks. They should be joint accounts in the bank with both names on them, but the checks in the checkbook could have just one name listed. The same would be true of individual savings account, joint accounts at the bank, individual names on the passbooks. In case of emergency, either spouse could withdraw monies from any account.

Years ago, my wife and I went to this system, and we have really enjoyed it. We have tried having a single checkbook where I kept the accounts. We have tried having a single checkbook where Cindy kept the accounts. We have tried several variations partly because my background involves working with a business. Because my father is a successful businessman, I felt I had a good grasp in financial practices, whereas my wife was a little less knowledgeable in those areas.

We experimented a little bit to find the right combination

which would allow us the greatest freedom with the least amount of controversy. Also, we wanted to maintain our independence as individuals.

Whatever income we receive is all given to me, and I take the responsibility to make the different deposits into my checking account and her checking account. In order to give her an appropriate allowance, we listed every expenditure that she has in the areas of her responsibilities. (In a later chapter, I will mention responsibilities in the home and what areas should belong to the husband and to the wife.)

My wife is a traditional housewife, and I am a traditional family man. I basically earn the income on which our family operates, and Cindy basically maintains the household duties. Cindy and I listed every expense she has as a housewife and as a mother. Some of the expenses we listed were:

- cleaning supplies
- groceries
- saving for remodeling
- repairing or replacing worn items
- buying clothing for our children
- school supplies
- gifts for teachers and classmates
- anniversary gifts for loved ones
- birthday gifts for loved ones
- Christmas gifts for loved ones
- personal items, etc.

We figured approximate prices for each item we listed, added all those different figures together, and then I added an additional ten percent to that number. That ten percent was for a margin of error as well as some money for her to use for discretionary spending—her own free money.

Each month, I take the amount that we decided plus the ten percent and deposit it into her account. Since I am paid twice monthly, that means I deposit 50 percent of her monthly allocation in her checking account twice a month. I give her the deposit slip for her checking account, and then she distributes the money as she sees fit. I don't check up on her, nor does she report to me. She simply takes care of her responsibilities.

I expect Cindy to provide food for the family, and I expect to have a good meal when I sit down to eat. I expect the children to be clothed properly, but I don't have to check on her. She has certainly earned my trust, and I love her, and I want her to feel she has a portion of the say-so and a portion of independence in our marriage.

From time to time, major expenses arise of which we were not aware. An emergency occurs or perhaps we want to plan a special vacation that is a little more expensive. We discuss those matters together as husband and wife or even as a family of four, and we formulate a plan to begin saving some extra money. On occasion, we might even open a separate savings account.

Part of the fun of purchasing an expensive, well-made piece of furniture or a major appliance or taking a special vacation is looking forward to it and saving for it.

Budgets

Every couple should have a simple budget to follow. The following is a simple, practical breakdown of how I recommend married couples to allocate their money. Of course, ten percent of the gross income is the tithe to the local church. That is life or death as well as mandatory because that ten percent is God's money. No one has a choice in the matter of whether or not he should tithe; it is a must. There must also be an offering for the work of the Lord through the local church. The amount is discretionary with each person, but certainly an offering of gratitude should be given at each pay period in addition to the tithe (ten percent of the gross amount from all sources). Consider the tithe a rent to God for use of His earth. The offering is a gift of love from you to Him.

I recommend that no more than 30 percent of a couple's income be used for a mortgage payment or rent. The mortgage payment should include homeowner's insurance and real estate taxes. If a couple is paying rent, they may want to consider purchasing renter's insurance. If so, the renter's insurance payment would be included in that 30 percent set aside for housing.

I recommend that 10 percent of the couple's income be set aside for utilities and repairs for the house.

I recommend 15 percent of the income to be allocated for groceries and household supplies, including cleaning and detergent materials.

I recommend 10 percent of the income to be saved for gifts (Christmas, anniversary, birthday, etc.) and family vacations. This money would be put into a savings account and drawn out as needed for the different times of the year when it is needed.

I recommend five percent of the couple's income should be placed in savings for investment purposes. Five percent is not a great amount, but it is a start. Many young couples fall prey to different scams and schemes, so I recommend avoiding any kind of offbeat idea that sounds too good to be true. The age-old adage will always be true, "If it sounds too good to be true, it usually is."

The remaining 20 percent should be used for miscellaneous bills such as a car payment or discretionary spending—a date, a new dress, or maybe something for a sport or a hobby in which both are involved.

The following is a chart to be used as a reminder:

Tithe 10%
Housing 30%
Utilities and repairs 10%
Groceries and household supplies 15%
Gifts 10%
Investment savings 5%
Miscellaneous .20%

Certainly, these percentages do not have to be absolute numbers. The only absolute number is the ten percent allocated to the tithe, God's money. Some items may have some variation in these numbers, and that would be understandable.

Allowances

As our children have gotten older, I can offer some advice that we have used that has helped us in our philosophy of finances. Our children do not have a weekly allowance. I am not a strong advocate of an allowance, though I am a strong advocate for rewarding hard work. Many added expenses have arisen for our children as they have become teenagers. Therefore, I have set up a separate savings account for Jaclynn and Kenny. Each month I deposit a set portion of our money into that savings account. Our children earn money by performing services that allow them to withdraw money from their savings account against the hours that they have worked. In this way, our children are not constantly coming to my wife or me asking us for nickel-and-dime things.

Let me reiterate that my entire philosophy is that I want to avoid the necessity of talking about our finances. I don't mind discussing the matter of finances with my wife; I just don't want to have to talk about them. When the finances are planned as I have suggested in this chapter, practically no time is spent in mandatory discussions about money. I believe the less time spent in discussing controversial subjects, the more likely a couple will have a happy home and a sweet, romantic marriage!

SIMPLE WAYS TO HELP SAVE MONEY

• **Shop once a week, and don't shop in between times.** It is a simple fact that every time a person goes to the store he will spend money. It stands to reason that the fewer trips an individual makes to the store, the less money he will spend. I recommend making a shopping list before going to the store—whether it is Wal-Mart, K-Mart, or a grocery store. Make a shopping list of what needs to be purchased; buy those items and nothing more.

• **Don't use unnecessary cleaning supplies.** Turn off the television advertisements that sound so good. Use simple products that work well. Check with those who have been cleaning for a long time and find out what products they use. Don't fall prey to the advertising moguls who are only after money.

• **Clip coupons.** It can be fun to do as a couple, and it will save a few dollars each week.

• **Shop at discount grocery stores.** The major chains often entice shoppers with discount items, but then have much higher prices for the basics that must be purchased weekly.

• **Shop at thrift shops, especially for casual clothing.** When purchasing everyday wear, don't shop at the major name-brand stores. Instead, go to Goodwill, Salvation Army, resale shops, and discount places. Many upper-middle class and wealthy people donate like-new, expensive clothing to those kinds of places. The wise shopper can purchase basic, classic, and otherwise expensive clothing for minimal prices.

• **Learn to send cards and letters rather than purchase expensive gifts for loved ones.** A homemade card, a homemade gift, a very thoughtful letter, or a card with a very thoughtful poem written inside is often much more meaningful than an expensive store-bought gift.

• **Learn to use stationery and inexpensive cards.** Writing a gift of words is often more meaningful than a store-bought gift.

• **Space out long-distance phone calls.** Call when rates are cheaper—in the evenings or on weekends.

• **Plan the phone time.** Don't just call on a whim, but make plans to call relatives or friends.

• **Learn something about the person's taste for whom a gift is being purchased.** Often, we spend far too much time and money purchasing items when we don't know what the person for whom we are buying wants or needs. Take 30 minutes and plan what should be bought for somebody. Study the person to discover what the person would like, rather than purchasing an expensive, unusable, and often unnecessary gift.

• **Give gifts on time.** As a rule, the longer a person waits to buy a gift (especially if purchased late), the more the person wants to salve his conscience by spending more money for the gift. Plan ahead!

• **Look for items that will stay in style for a long time.** The wise shopper will not fall prey to the fads and trends. Buy the basic, prudent styles that are sharp and in style but that are not faddish or trendy.

• **Look a long time before buying.** Don't give in to the urge to buy and become a compulsive buyer. That urge is so dangerous, and it will put a couple in debt so quickly especially if they have that "plastic wizard" called a credit card. Ungoverned spending will seriously hurt a marriage.

• **Schedule luxury.** For example, cook a big dinner once a week, and cook small meals the rest of the week.

• **Plan when to have a splurge.** A couple should plan a splurge in advance so they can look for bargains at the store. By no means should every night be a splurge.

• **A couple should learn to do things for themselves.** The library is full of "how-to" books that teach gardening, carpet cleaning, or repairing small household items. Just getting a car washed at the automatic car wash can cost four to ten dollars. Instead, wash the car together at the house.

• **Don't window shop.** The only way I would consider window shopping is if I left my cash, my checks, and my credit cards at home. I would not trust myself otherwise. Most people cannot afford to window shop because they cannot resist buying even some things they never knew existed!

❦

Finally, let me address an issue to which I have alluded in these previous points—credit cards. Today, charge cards are available to almost anyone who can fill out an application. I understand that it is almost impossible to function as a traveler or to take a vacation without needing to use a credit card. If my wife and I were a young couple getting married right now, I would put our credit cards in an inaccessible place. I advise others to do the same thing.

It is unwise to carry charge cards on a daily basis; and by all means, credit cards should not be used for purchasing daily basic items such as groceries, casual wear, or basic needs.

If the charge card is needed for a vacation or for traveling, I understand that, but the wise couple will use their charge card for that reason only. They ought to pay off what has been charged immediately so as not to incur a high interest rate charge. Interest charges can financially bury a couple in debt and thereby forfeit their privilege and responsibility of caring for dreams on their future wish list.

Because I believe the topic of finances to be of such great importance regarding the health of a marriage, I have put together a complete financial series on tape and in booklets. I strongly suggest for couples to obtain the tapes and booklets and to become experts at getting out of debt, staying out of debt, and knowing how to obtain God's blessings through the wise use of money. You may obtain this series, *God's Plan for Your Money*, by writing to Hyles Publications, 523 Sibley Street, Hammond, Indiana, 46320.

⌒ℐ

Checklist and Review

1. The old axiom, "If everybody is in charge, then ___ is in charge," can be applied to handling money in marriage.

2. God has definite principles for finances in marriage:
   a. ___ the money.
   b. ___ the money.
   c. ___ the item.

3. The person designated to be in charge of the family finances should budget an ___ for his/her spouse.

4. A couple should build their financial principle around the philosophy, "I do not want to ___ to talk about the finances."

5. List at least five ways to save money.

SEVEN

A Delicate Subject

PROBABLY THE MOST controversial subject I address in pre-marital counseling is the topic of birth control. I realize that every person has his own opinion, as do his friends, parents, doctors, and his counselors. Allow me to share the following thoughts from my heart about this delicate subject.

God has given a couple a tremendous power, the power to produce a never-dying, eternal soul. That power, prior to Adam and Eve, was reserved only for God. He chose to share that power with us, and we truly are joint-heirs with Him in the production of life. *"Likewise, ye husbands, dwell with them according to knowledge, giving honour unto the wife, as unto the weaker vessel, and as being heirs together of the grace of life; that your prayers be not hindered."* (I Peter 3:7)

Simply having a power does not give us the right to use it as we freely decide, nor is it wise to simply reassign that power to God's providential care. It is true that God can intervene anytime He chooses, but God has chosen to give each of us wisdom and understanding to use the powers that He has provided.

Think of that power as the ability of an automobile to transport people from place to place. If an individual has an automobile, he has the right and power as a licensed driver to operate that vehicle. Though he has that power and that right, he does not have the license to make up his own rules or drive in a way that is outside the limits of common sense. Otherwise, lives might be endangered. Therefore, strict laws govern the use of an individual's rights.

Also, it would be foolish to get into a car and just sit there expecting and waiting for God to start the car and then drive us from point "A" to point "B." God is a very practical God. He wants a person to use the brain He has been given to plan his life and to live his life according to His will, His precepts, and His commands. With these thoughts in mind, let me share four points about the subject of birth control.

1. Marriage is the most important relationship. When God placed Adam and Eve in the garden of Eden, He put them there as a husband and wife, not as a father and child, not as a mother and child, and not as a single man or woman alone. In fact, for a brief time, Adam was alone. *"And the LORD God said, It is not good that the man should be alone; I will make him an help meet for him."* (Genesis 2:18) From the beginning, God's opinion of the single life was that it was not good.

God's will for nearly every person is that he should marry. His will for nearly every married couple is that they should have children. Psalm 127:3 says, *"Lo, children are an heritage of the LORD: and the fruit of the womb is his reward."* Children are a gift from God; however, the foundation of our society is a husband and a wife, who in their love and wisdom, bring children into this world. Children added to a weak and unstable marriage multiply the problems in the marriage. Having children you do not want or are unprepared to nurture is unfair to the child and unwise for the marriage. Probably there is no greater home wrecker than a child. Please don't misunderstand me. Children are the greatest joy and delight to a married couple. However, children brought into this world when the marriage is full of strife and contention can only amplify that strife and produce greater contention. Many a marriage has failed when sweet, precious children have come into a home where there is an unstable marriage. Every couple should make their marriage the most important concern.

2. What is right for both the husband and the wife is right for the marriage. Two people will undoubtedly have differing opinions on how many children to have and how to rear those children. I believe it is very important for a couple to decide in general terms how many children to have. Perhaps the husband came from a large family, so he thinks six or more children is the right number. On the other hand, perhaps the wife has seen a mother travail with children, or she has seen a difficult home life. As a result, she feels that too many children can be a burden to a family.

I highly recommend that a couple write down on a piece of paper the number of children each one would like to have. They should then compare those numbers, discuss them simply, and come to some type of agreement or compromise.

If the couple cannot agree on the number, I personally believe that the wife should have the final say-so for the very simple reason that she is the one who has to bear the children. She has to go through the turmoil, the travail, the pain, and the suffering of bringing a child into this world. Since a husband's role in that nine-month pregnancy period is minimal, the wife should make the decision as to when the children are born. Certainly I am not advocating a wife controlling a marriage or telling her husband what to do. I simply believe that a couple should discuss this matter, and if they cannot come to a mutual understanding at this particular time, the wife should have the vote.

3. Develop and cultivate the right kind of romantic love. A husband must realize that his wife feels very insecure if every romantic rendezvous might produce a child. Oftentimes, a couple will come to me for counseling with the husband disappointed with the romantic physical union.

He thinks the wife should have been more open in her affection and that she is holding back. In reality, his wife is not affectionate and loving because she is scared to death that they are going to conceive a baby as a result of a romantic time. Therefore, the wife is withdrawn and tends to be overly cautious about giving herself freely to her husband.

I believe that a marriage must get off to a good solid beginning. If a newly-married couple is older (late twenties or early thirties), I don't believe that there is any particular need to wait a lengthy amount of time to bring children into the world. Especially is this true if the couple is solid, emotionally stable, and spiritual. However, the traditional young couple in their early twenties should allow some time for their marriage to develop and mature before they have children. I normally suggest that a couple wait at least one year before they attempt to have children. This wait would give them nearly two years with each other before a child enters the home.

I realize this openly sexual age in which we live advocates free talk about the intimate marital relationship on the radio and television. Jokes and lewdness are openly and freely discussed among family members and friends. It seems everyone pretends to be an expert on romantic love. The actual physical act of romantic love is very easy to learn; however, the love making of a tender husband and an affectionate wife with the proper expressions and the aura and atmosphere that go into a solid, loving, stable home takes many years to develop properly.

When I was engaged, I picked up a book on marriage by a well-known author who said that the act of marriage takes 25 years to learn to master. I put down the book and thought, "That poor soul. He is an older man who has a boring wife and marriage." At the time, I did not realize that he was writing some excellent, wise material. It is fun to make love from day one, and the intimate marital relationship can be wonderful. However, reality tells me, as a marriage counselor, that very few couples start off on day one with all of the fulfillment and joy that they had fantasized would be there.

I have been married 23 years, and I must now agree with that author. Our relationship has only been an increasingly more delightful journey—a wonderful adventure to a more fully developed romantic love that every couple is allowed by the grace of God. Having children right away could preempt further development and could interfere with a couple getting off to a good, solid romantic love relationship. Therefore, I recommend the postponing of having children for some time.

4. If a couple decides to postpone having children, some means or methods to postpone having a child will need to be utilized. Many fine Christian men and women believe any kind of birth control is wrong. They feel that having a child should be left in the hands of God.

However, I have been in many housing project areas where scores and scores of mothers live in a house with several children and no husband to care for them. I see the product and fruit of complete disregard for any common sense as to bringing children into this world. Again, simply having the power to have a child does not give any person the permission to use it at his discretion. If God was going to intervene, He simply would intervene with these people who have no regard for morality or decency. He does not because He has given to each of us that power to use at our own discretion. Like any responsibility—whether it is money, a job opportunity, or a material possession—God gives us those responsibilities and asks us to use His wisdom and common-sense, practical principles from His Word to govern them.

I believe the couple should read books about birth control. Certainly, it is not wrong to seek the advice of trusted counselors; both will want to talk to their marriage counselor about this very matter.

When choosing birth control, I recommend that the wife-to-be should have a very frank discussion with her doctor four to six months before her wedding date about all the avenues available. It is true that some birth control measures actually are a form of abortion, and I would definitely not want to see any couple choose those methods. However, there are some safe, common-sense methods that should be discussed with a trusted medical doctor who loves God and has the couple's best interests at heart. Some birth control methods require a three-month time frame to begin to work effectively in a woman's system.

I also recommend that an engaged couple have a very brief but planned discussion about birth control approximately three months before the wedding date. The couple should not discuss the mechanics of the intimate marital relationship. They should not discuss the first night of the honeymoon or married love. This discussion should be professional and brief about what each feels is wise and practical for them in the area of birth control.

The couple should keep in mind that parents and friends will have their opinions. I advise couples to also keep in mind that moms and dads have a right to their opinions, and they have a right to want to guide their children along certain lines. For the most part, however, they have had their opportunity for rearing and training. Therefore, I recommend that the couple decide what the two of them want. They also should seek some good medical advice so they do not make a decision based on ignorance, tradition, fear, peer pressure, or parental pressure. The couple should make their decision only when they understand all of the options, when they understand what the doctor is advising, and when they feel they know what choice is the right one for them. Once that decision is made, what has been decided is no one else's business.

My personal thoughts on birth control are very simple. I believe a couple should utilize the safest and easiest method available. Some methods are 80 percent effective; some have higher percentages of effectiveness. I recommend using the safest method the couple agrees is proper with their level of understanding and with their marriage in mind.

When I counsel with an engaged couple, I tell them what I have just written, but I also tell them that I do not need to know what their decision is. I am a counselor. I am a guide. I am an advisor, but I am not a manipulator of the will of God in their lives. I do not have to live with the children that they choose to bring into this world, nor do I have to live with the decisions they have made. I simply offer them, in this case, some options and some choices. I answer a few of their personal questions, and then I leave the decision of birth control to them.

❧

Checklist and Review

1. Having the power to create a never-dying soul does not give any person the ___ to use that power as he so decides.

2. In the same respect, to attribute that power to the providence of God is not always ___.

3. The problems in an unstable marriage are ___ when children are added.

4. It is ___ to a child when he is unwanted or if the couple is unprepared to nurture him.

5. The most important relationship is ___.

6. Approximately three months before the wedding date, the couple should have a brief but ___ discussion about birth control.

EIGHT

Household Duties and Chores

WE TEND TO think that marriages most often end in divorce court because of an extramarital affair or because of some horrendous sin committed by one of the marital partners. Instead, I have found a marriage usually flounders because of the little nibbling, biting, and fussing that breaks down the foundation of the marriage. Usually the undermining of a marriage is over matters like the following:

- Who will take care of a broken window?
- Who will fix the muffler on the car? Since, there is no money to do it, how will the car be fixed?
- Who will sweep out the garage?
- Who will take out the trash?
- Who will mop the floors?
- Since we both work full time, who will fix the evening meals?

On and on the list goes. The little, petty grievances that nibble and bite eventually cause the marriage to be so weakened that it is devoured. Then, that marriage becomes an easy victim for what we term a big problem, such as adultery.

I believe the most important point in maintaining household duties and chores is to make a priority list. The couple should weigh what **needs** to be done versus what they would *like* to have done. Therefore, each couple should make a "must-do list" and a "wish list." A "must-do" list contains chores that must be done. A wish list contains items the couple would like to be able to do in the house should they have money and the time.

Certainly, a wish list is fun to make. However, I believe finances should determine the timing of when those wishes are realized. For instance, I have a wish list; it happens to be a page in my little prayer book that I refer to in my private prayer time with God. On my wish list, I have listed a new driveway which will cost about $1,800. Since I don't have that allotted extra money, I am praying about it and saving some money in my savings account each month. I want to do some landscaping on our lawn. I would also like to build a little gazebo with a terrace and garden for my wife. Since that wish will take more money than I have at this time, I am waiting on that particular wish. The linoleum in our kitchen needs replacing; again, I am saving for that expense. We can live without any of the items on my wish list; when and if we fulfill any of our wishes will be determined by our financial ability.

Those are some examples on my wish list. No doubt every couple would have different items on their lists. I believe once the couple has decided what their "must-do" list is, then they should determine item by item who will be responsible for each.

- Decide who will do the dishes.
- Decide who will repair the gutters.
- Decide who will care for the car repairs.
- Decide who will care for changing light bulbs.
- Decide who will clean the windows.
- Decide who will do the spring cleaning.
- Decide who will clean the basement.

- Decide who will clean the garage.
- Decide who will organize the attic.
- Decide who will rearrange dresser drawers.
- Decide who will care for the appliances when they break down.
- Decide who will care for the vacuuming, sweeping and mopping.
- Decide who will fix the glides on the dresser drawers when they break.
- Decide who will tighten the knobs on dressers or tighten the handles on the pots and pans.
- Decide who takes care of cleaning the oven, washing out the refrigerator and organizing the hall closet.

All of these little details should be assigned to the husband or the wife. It is far too easy to just assume, "It's his responsibility or hers." The problem is that in most marriages the couple knows who will do it—the other one. Once again both husband and wife believe the other is in charge, and so, neither is in charge. The job is only cared for when the problem becomes a disaster. Then bitterness, anger, and frustration result. This problem seems too trivial even to address, yet it is the nitty gritty of life. These are the hundreds of little, trivial responsibilities that make up life, and someone has to be responsible for them.

Therefore, the couple should make a list of all of their responsibilities while thinking of every practical thing that went wrong in their parents' house as they grew up. Both the husband and wife should write down those items. After the list is complete, the couple should set it aside for a couple of weeks. On another date, they should continue to add to that list. Over the next couple of months, as the couple continues to plan and prepare for their wedding day, they should take out that list frequently and add to it or reorganize it. When the list is about as thorough and complete as it possibly can be, the couple should get together and go through each item and ask, "Who will take care of this?" The ideal is to decide who will do what before the wedding day. By so doing, all of those areas of responsibilities which so easily become points of contention are cared for ahead of time.

For instance, when the trash is not taken out, and the list dictates the husband is going to take it out, it remains the husband's responsibility. His wife won't have to wonder who is in charge. If the trash is piled so high that the family is tripping over it, the wife can sweetly say, "I think that this is your responsibility," and she is right. Together the couple decided ahead of time who would be responsible. At the same time, the couple gave each other permission to be responsible for their items.

Suppose the husband is assigned to do minor household repairs. Whether he does it himself or hires a handyman or an expert, I believe the most important thing is to decide before the wedding day how to communicate with each other about these repairs. It is a bad scenario when a husband comes home from a busy day at work, and his wife greets him with a list of needed repairs. He begins to feel that he is nothing more than a handyman and that he has lost his right to be her man, her lover, her friend, and her companion. No husband wants to be nothing more than the hired man who only does chores around the house and runs errands.

Likewise, if a wife, out of financial necessity, works outside of the home to help with the income, she doesn't want to be greeted with a list of "to-do's" when she gets home from work. Since she has a job and her husband has a job perhaps on a different shift, all he does is remind her of all the things that need to be cared for in her areas of responsibility.

Before they know it, the couple begins discussing what they do not like about each other and how unhappy they are with the place in which they live. The couple develops a negative mentality about what is wrong with their house, what is wrong with their marriage, and what is wrong with each other. They harbor bitter feelings.

In our home, I have asked Cindy to make a short list for me on a weekly basis. At my request, she attaches that list to the mirror where I shave each morning. We never discuss it because we do not need to discuss it. I promised Cindy that anything she writes on that list will be cared for within seven days. If it is an item that is financially impossible for me to accomplish within seven days, I give her an approximate time frame that I believe I can care for the matter.

My wife knows that if a bulb burns out or a window breaks or the gutters are plugged, within seven days it will be fixed, whether I have to fix it myself or call a repairman. For any major item of expense, within seven days, I give her a workable timetable of when I believe it can be fixed. If the item is not cared for after seven days, I give my wife permission to call a repairman, and I will pay for the expense. This motivates me to care for the problems and gives her security that she will be cared for.

The idea is to avoid the necessity of having to discuss these controversial matters. Sure, a couple may talk about anything they choose, but why talk about who didn't take out the trash and who didn't change the lightbulb? I would like to think that a couple would rather turn on some nice music and relax with sweet conversation. Surely, anything is better than having to talk about how disappointed he is over the fact that she isn't doing what he assumed she would be doing or vice versa. How wise it is to take care of all the assumptions before marriage! Then a couple can live out marriage according to a plan they have chosen and agreed upon prior to the wedding day.

ᐤ

Checklist and Review

1. Usually the bickering that arises from the little situations of marriage undermine it and cause the marriage to ___.

2. A wise couple compiles a "must-do" list for their home and then decides item by item who will be ___ for each item.

3. Deciding who will do what chores avoids the ___ of having to discuss matters that might well become controversial.

NINE

Child Rearing

IBELIEVE THAT BEFORE marriage it is important for a couple to settle a few basic issues of child rearing so as not to bring disappointment when this crucial time of transition arrives.

1. **The single most helpful decision in rearing children is to put them on a schedule.** Some modern psychologists of the last quarter century appeared to support the idea that children themselves should basically run the home. I believe the parents should maintain the control, set the schedule, and make the child conform to their schedule—not vice versa.

Please don't misunderstand me. Infants have incredible needs, and parental attention will be required every couple of hours for feeding and bathing and cleansing. However, I strongly believe a schedule is vital to maintain equilibrium, stability, and happiness in the home, especially between the parents.

A lady named Gladys West Hendrick wrote an outstanding book entitled *My First 300 Babies*. No, she herself did not have 300 babies, but she was hired by many families to come into their homes, set up their nurseries, and help put the children on a schedule. My wife and I bought a copy of this book before we had our first child, and we owe this lady a tremendous debt. I believe the book is "must" reading. I encourage every couple with whom I counsel to buy the book.

In addition, some other outstanding books to read would be Dr. John R. Rice's book, *The Home: Courtship and Marriage,* and Dr. Jack Hyles' books on *How to Rear Infants, How to Rear Children,* and *How to Rear Teenagers.* Dr. Rice's book is available through *The Sword of the Lord* Publishers in Murfreesboro, Tennessee, and Dr. Jack Hyles' books are available through Hyles Publications in Hammond, Indiana.

2. A couple should decide who will discipline the children and when the children will be disciplined. Personally, I believe when a child commits an infraction, the parent who sees the rule being broken should discipline the child. However, if Mom and Dad are both home, I believe the father should take the initiative in caring for the children. I strongly believe it is unfair to a child and to the father if the mother sees the child commit an infraction of the rules and then says, "Wait until Daddy gets home. He'll spank you then."

That kind of disciplinary method causes the child to dread the father's coming home when his arrival should be a happy time. I believe that discipline should be meted out immediately by the parent who sees the infraction.

I believe it is wise to decide a few basic rules on what age the children will be disciplined. My wife and I decided that we would begin to reprimand our children when they were mobile on their own. In other words, we began to discipline them when they began to crawl. In our minds, they were able to make their own decisions about where they went and how they got there, and they were expressing their own wills.

3. I would recommend that every couple decide some basic rights and wrongs for their children. Before

Cindy and I got married, we decided what absolute wrongs or rights we would have for our children. We also decided why we would spank. We came up with a list of seven absolutes which included lying, fighting with their siblings, talking back to parents, etc. Every couple should make a list of those major offenses for which their children should be disciplined.

4. Every couple should have family vacations for their family only. No wise couple will take friends or even other relatives on their regular outings. The family unit needs to be strengthened and built on vacations as well as during family times. We had a family motto for years: "Us four and no more." We lived by that motto to keep our family unit strong.

5. The wise couple will schedule time each week to be with each child. In a traditional family, the mother will automatically spend more time with the children than the father does. Therefore, the father should have special times with each child each week. This should be scheduled time so the children can count on his being with them. The father should plan to do a variety of activities.

- Teach the child to work.
- Teach the child to read.
- Play with the child.
- Take the child to places of interest.

I am not even advocating spending money on them necessarily. I am recommending being with the child. The average father spends less than two minutes per day with his children. This a tragic fact that should not be true in Christian homes.

6. The wise couple will use baby-sitters. A marriage continues just like it started: The husband won his wife's heart while dating. The wise couple will keep alive that same dating and romance—buying gifts, sending flowers, sending cards, writing sweet poems, and making phone calls in the middle of the day. All of these will cause the romance to thrive.

The children should not rob a couple of their romance and free time with each other. Most couples do not like to place their infant's care in the hands of a baby-sitter. Trust me, for the sake of the marriage, do it. Reputable baby-sitters can be found by checking with people who have used them. Find one who is reliable. It is so important to have a date at least once a week.

⟨∾⟩

We cannot consider this chapter to be a comprehensive study on child rearing. I trust that the few thoughts presented will whet the appetite for further study and help a couple get off to a good start during the transition from married life into the early days of child rearing.

RECOMMENDED FURTHER READING
How to Rear Infants by Dr. Jack Hyles
How to Rear Children by Dr. Jack Hyles
How to Rear Teenagers by Dr. Jack Hyles
Making Wise the Simple by Dr. Jack Schaap
Rearing Kids with Character by Pete and Frieda Cowling

⟨∾⟩

Checklist and Review

1. Putting a child on a ___ is probably the wisest decision a couple can make in regard to rearing children.

2. A ___ is crucial in maintaining and promoting calmness, stability, and happiness in the home.

3. Because a marriage needs consistent nurturing, the wise couple will make use of ___, within reason.

4. When a child breaks a rule, the parent who sees the rule being broken should ___ the child.

TEN

Dreams and Goals

A N ENGAGED COUPLE should consider their work dreams or their goals and visions for their life both personally and together. It is amazing to me that a couple can fall in love and never really know where they are headed and what each really wants out of life. Most never know what each feels he wants to accomplish by retirement age.

I am not merely addressing financial stability; I am addressing visionary goals. God placed every person on this earth for a purpose. For that reason, when I counsel with an engaged couple, I always ask a series of questions:

- What would you like to do in your lifetime?
- Do you know what that purpose is?
- Do you know how to accomplish your purpose?
- Do you have a vision of what God would like you to do with your life?

That vision of what God would like a person to do with his life is called the will of God. Every person ought to know what the will of God is for his life. I advise an engaged couple to have a time together, perhaps a date, to write out the four or five big goals they have in mind for their future together.

On occasion, each member of my family and I write out

100 things we would like to do before we die. Some of the things on our lists are:

- Read a certain book.
- Visit a certain place.
- Vacation in an exotic place.
- Play a certain sport.
- Learn a certain game.
- Own a particular car/truck.
- Work a certain job.
- Work in a certain position at the job.
- Teach a certain age Sunday school class.
- Build a big church bus route.
- Eat a food that has never been tried.

Cindy, Jaclynn, Kenny, and I have a lot of fun making our lists and comparing them. I find it amazing how many things we have already done on our lists, and we like to add to them from time to time.

Let me establish a couple of principles that have a direct influence on attaining those dreams and goals.

1. A woman finds her security in her husband, her family, and her household.

2. A man finds his security and his self-value in his work. Therefore, every lady needs to understand that his job is very important to him. A wife must give her husband the freedom to succeed at his job.

A wife wants her husband to succeed without his leaving her behind. Many times a job becomes a threat to a wife because she feels that she is being pushed out as her husband's time and attention are focused on his job. When the husband is with his wife, he is often a tired, grumpy man who is worn out from his job. Instead of becoming a delight and a joy to her, the job becomes a threat—almost an enemy to her. However, every lady must keep in mind that a job is a man's security, and he finds his dignity in his ability to work and provide.

A tug of war often occurs between the job and the wife, but I believe much of this could be prevented if the couple would share their dreams and goals before marriage. A couple needs to share with each other a simple plan of what they think the Lord wants them to do, and they should outline how they think those goals and dreams might be fulfilled. Certainly, we do not pretend to know what God will do ahead of time, but it is wonderful for a person to have a vision and to know why he is here on this earth.

In Proverbs 24:27, the Bible says, *"Prepare thy work without, and make it fit for thyself in the field; and afterwards build thine house."* I believe this verse teaches that a person should figure out what God wants him to do on this earth, be prepared to do it, and then establish a marriage and family. It is difficult for a wife to feel security when her husband is too lazy to get a job. How can a wife be a helpmeet, helping her husband succeed, when he is going nowhere?

I believe the best way to become close and intimate is to get into a yoke. By that I mean, a married couple should be pulling together in the same direction, i.e., going the same direction in life, having a vision, and being determined to make something of their lives.

Having dreams and goals can be used as inspiration on difficult days when the drudgery of life becomes a little monotonous. How can two walk together if neither has any desire to go anywhere? When I counsel teenagers and young adults who are seriously dating, I insist on their not getting married until after they have decided, at the very least, a general course for life. How can a wife help her husband to succeed if she doesn't know where he is going in life?

⁓

Checklist and Review

1. What God would like a person to do with his life is commonly called the ___ .

2. A ___ finds her security in her ___ , her ___ , and her ___ .

3. A ___ finds his security and his self-value in his ___ .

4. At times, a wife views her husband's ___ as a threat because his attentions are focused elsewhere.

5. One way a married couple can become close and intimate is by ___ .

ELEVEN

Having a Personal Relationship with God

PERHAPS THE MOST easily neglected part of married life is a couple's personal relationship with the Lord Jesus Christ—as individuals, as a couple, and eventually as a family. It is so important for a couple to decide ahead of time that their marriage will be one having spiritual depth and influence.

Usually, when I travel somewhere and speak, I stay in a motel room. That room is a new environment where I will spend the next two or three days. Out of necessity, that room has to become my home for those days. I cannot allow myself to indulge in some improper behavior or to become disoriented, thus neglecting my personal habits that keep me right with God.

One of the first things that I do when I go into a motel room is to decide where I am going to pray and where I am going to read my Bible. Perhaps this sounds trivial or trite, but I want to be sure that I do those things that keep me in a close harmony with my God.

As a couple contemplates marriage, they need to decide what kind of personal daily relationship they will have with God. A couple cannot afford to neglect Him nor ignore Him lest they find themselves without His daily blessing, guidance, and spiritual help. With this introduction in mind, let me share a few thoughts about staying in harmony with God.

1. Every person should have a place where he will read his Bible. A person cannot read the Bible once a month or a few times a year and be spiritually minded. Every person should get into the discipline of reading the Bible every day. Every person should have a special place to read the Bible.

In every home, there is a place to eat, a place to sleep, a place to entertain, a place to bathe, a place to put away clothing, and a place to store the vacuum cleaner. There is a place for everything. The old adage, "A place for everything, and everything in its place," is the great secret to an organized life.

I must ask, "Where do you read your Bible?" Since most people don't have a designated place, most people don't read their Bibles. My wife and I have different places where we read our Bibles. I read my Bible at the kitchen table or on my knees at our bedside, and Cindy reads her Bible in an overstuffed chair in our living room. Just as we have our places to read the Bible, so must every other person.

2. Every person should have a time to read the Bible. The same is true for prayer, and everything else that relates to the Christian life. Just as a couple has a set time for meals and for work, so must the Christian have a set time for the spiritual.

For instance, our supper time is at 5:30 p.m. every night. Our breakfast time is 6:30 a.m. every morning. I must be at work at 7:45 a.m. for a special meeting every morning; most mornings I get there much earlier. If every person would be as disciplined and as diligent in having a time to pray as he is in having a time to eat, a time to bathe, a time to get dressed, a time for a date, and a time to go to work, then he would be faithful in his Bible reading and prayer time. When a person's walk with God is as consistent as eating and working, he will begin seeing that discipline pays off in his personal walk with God.

3. Every person should use a Bible reading schedule. Often I am asked how much Bible one should read. Don't read a verse or two in haste, but follow a good schedule. I strongly recommend that you read through the Bible at least one time each year. Reading three chapters every day will accomplish that goal. That only requires about 10-15 minutes per day. Also, I suggest you read until your heart warms to the truths you are reading, but at least read by schedule.

The Bible contains the very Words of God. The Bible is a personal love letter written to every person by God Himself, and I want every Christian to read it until he gets a verse or a phrase or words that warm his heart. I don't even mean hours and hours—only a few have time to do that. Every person should set aside some time, at least 15 to 20 minutes and preferably 30 minutes, where he reads until God's Word begins to speak to his heart.

4. Every person should make a prayer list. I have a little three-by-five inch spiral bound notebook that I keep in my shirt pocket. Every time I hear a special prayer request, I write it down in my notebook. I list the names of my family, loved ones, my church, our deacons, and our Sunday school teachers, to name a few of the people in my notebook. I list special requests in no particular order as I hear them or as I think of them. As a minimum, every day in my prayer closet, I pray for one full notebook page of prayer requests. If one page has only a dozen or so items listed, I may have time to pray for two pages of requests. Sometimes I will linger on one or two items a little longer as I feel a particular burden in my heart to do so, but I always get through at least one page on my prayer list every day.

I do not get bogged down with having to go through my entire prayer list each day. Neither do I get bogged down in praying for the same requests over and over or by feeling like I am in a rut. My prayer life does not become meaningless; it stays fresh.

I have learned that prayer requires consistency. I believe a Christian should pray every day even on vacations and during holidays. I believe God belongs in one's life every single day. We cannot live without His blessings, so I recommend that every Christian try to have a sweet, personal relationship with Him.

Give God the best time of your day, and He'll make the best of your day.

Checklist and Review

1. When a couple forgets God, as individuals and as a couple, the result can be the loss of God's daily ___, ___, and ___.

2. In order to be disciplined in daily Bible reading, a person needs to have a ___ and a ___ where he reads his Bible.

3. Since the Bible is God's love letter to His children, every Christian should read until his heart is ___.

4. Having a prayer list will keep a Christian's prayer life ___ so that his prayer time will not become meaningless.

TWELVE

Church Attendance

A s a family, decisions need to be made about church attendance. Personally, I am a Sunday morning, Sunday night, and a Wednesday evening mid-week service person. I believe very strongly in the words of the famous preacher, Dr. Lee Roberson, whose axiom, "It takes three to thrive," is oft quoted. By that statement, of course, he means that it takes three services—Sunday morning, Sunday night, and Wednesday night—to thrive as a Christian. His advice is great. I have rarely found a faithful-to-church Christian who has greatly backslidden in his Christian walk. It is difficult for any Christian to get away from God when he is hearing good preaching from a man of God and when he is around the people of God on a regular basis.

I advise an engaged couple to decide before marriage that they won't even question about going to church after they are married. I believe it is a big mistake for a couple to get up on a Sunday morning (even if they have been up late the previous night) and say, "Well, I am not feeling so good. How about you? Do you think we should go to church?" If a couple starts questioning on Sunday morning, Sunday night, or even Wednesday night whether or not they should attend church, they will start finding excuses that they believe are important enough to keep them from the house of God. Don't you do that! You need to be in the church services.

I do not take the time to counsel a couple about their upcoming marriage if they will not promise me that they will be faithful to the house of God, the local church. Of course, that house of God should be a Bible-preaching, Bible-believing church that believes and promotes soul winning, living for others, strong Bible standards, and evangelizing the lost. A preacher should be in the pulpit who preaches firmly yet lovingly. The engaged couple needs to decide before marriage that church will be a central part of their marriage. *"But seek ye first the kingdom of God, and his righteousness; and all these things shall be added unto you."* (Matthew 6:33) Once made, a couple should never reopen that decision.

Invariably, as children come into the marriage and become an integral part of the family, parents will find 101 excuses as to why the children should not go to a church service. Occasionally, one parent may have to stay home with a sick child. However, if a constant problem arises with an ill child, the couple should try to find a baby-sitter or take turns watching the child. I really believe the family needs to be in church every time the doors are open. I also believe that a child should be in church as soon as he is old enough to be brought home from the hospital. The baby should be put in the nursery. That child should grow up in church from the infants' bed baby nursery all the way through his adult Sunday school years. Parents teach more by their consistent faithful attendance to church than by nearly anything else they teach their child.

Let me reiterate that every person should be involved in his local church. He should do more than just attend and be a spectator; he needs to be an active participant. If the church has a women's missionary society, the wife should join. If there is an adult couples Sunday school class for their age group, the couple should join and get involved. A couple should be willing to offer support to their teacher in any way they can, such as helping with planning, organizing, and assisting with activities. Both husband and wife should be in some kind of soul-winning program of the church.

The husband and wife should tell the pastor that they are willing to help in any capacity when help is needed. If the church has bus routes (as it should), a married couple could volunteer to work as bus workers. The husband could obtain his CDL license and become a bus driver. I cannot stress how important it is for a couple to become an integral part of a local church and not be mere spectators from the grandstands.

Time and time again, I work with single young adults who love their preacher, who love their church, who love their Sunday school teacher, who are faithful to the services, who come to the Sunday school activities, who meet, date, court, and fall in love. Soon, their relationship becomes serious, preparations for the wedding bells start, and the couple gets married.

Suddenly, this husband and wife who have been faithful in church now have their own little house in which to live. They have their own little schedule, their independence, and their freedom to come and go as they please without anyone checking on them. Often the newlywed couple begins to backslide terribly. Without meaning to, they become very inconsistent in their church attendance. If they do happen to come, they slide in the back door after the preaching has begun. They often miss the church service as they duck out early like honeymooners are typically known to do. As a result, they miss the fellowship of Christian brothers and sisters. Next, they usually stop attending their Sunday school class and start attending the pastor's class where they can get lost in the crowd. They stop going to activities, and they no longer volunteer for any work. They become what I call part-time, uninvolved spectators sitting high up in the bleacher seats—almost ignoring the game. I cannot begin to stress what a big mistake that couple is making.

Because I have watched this type of heartbreak over and over, I teach an engaged couple that decisions need to be made about church attendance before the marriage. Couples need to determine in their hearts that church will play a major and important role in their family. You will not have the marriage you desire or that God desires you to have unless your marriage is built on the solid foundation of faithful church attendance and faithful church involvement.

ᓂᓇ

Checklist and Review

1. In order for a Christian not to backslide, he must remain ___ to all of the services of the church.

2. Church must play a ___ part in the lives of an engaged couple to ensure the greatest potential of having a good marriage.

3. The parents' ___ trains a child for consistent church attendance more than anything else a parent does.

4. In the young married couple's life, that something "new" which if not checked will allow them the easiest avenue to withdraw from church is their own ___.

THIRTEEN

Soul Winning

SOUL WINNING IS telling others how to be born again by giving the Gospel to the unsaved. Mark 16:15 says, *"And he (Jesus) said unto them, Go ye into all the world, and preach the gospel to every creature."* The Bible teaches that Christians are to be soul winners. Whether going soul winning with another bus worker or with a soul-winning club or as a couple with their Sunday school class, a husband and wife team should go and be in an organized soul-winning ministry. Before choosing a soul-winning ministry, the couple would be wise to visit the different ministries the local church offers.

The Bible teaches that a Christian is not obedient and close to the heart of God if he is not a soul winner. *"Go ye therefore, and teach all nations, baptizing them in the name of the Father, and of the Son, and of the Holy Ghost: Teaching them to observe all things whatsoever I have commanded you: and, lo, I am with you alway, even unto the end of the world. Amen."* (Matthew 28:19, 20) Jesus was saying, "You go and preach the Gospel, and I will be with you." When Jesus "walks" with a Christian, that Christian will know the wonderful presence of God like he has never before known. The soul winner will have wonderful blessings on his life. When soul winning is placed as the top priority and activity in a Christian's life, he will have wisdom and power.

Without any equivocation, I would tell the Christian who has a bowling league which interferes with soul winning to ditch his bowling league and become a soul winner. If a Saturday golf outing with buddies interferes with soul winning, the Christian should find another time to go golfing, or he should give up golfing to go soul winning. Jesus said in Matthew 6:33, *"But seek ye first the kingdom of God, and his righteousness; and all these things shall be added unto you."* That verse teaches the principle that church and the activities surrounding church should be first priority over the different institutions, societies, and clubs to which a Christian belongs. Soul winning should be first priority over the activities, hobbies, and sports in which a Christian engages. Brothers and sisters in Christ at church should be first among all of the friends that a Christian has at work or in the neighborhood. The Bible should be first priority over all of the books, newspapers, and magazines a Christian reads. Prayer should be first priority over all the intimate relationships a Christian has with friends and loved ones.

A Christian must make God first in his life. The Lord Jesus Christ must have the preeminence in the Christian home. The Christian must ask himself:

- "Is my entertainment right with God?"
- "Would it be pleasing for Christ to see what I watch on the television screen?"
- "Would what I listen to on the radio be pleasing to Christ?"
- "Would Christ be pleased to hear the way I talk in my house?"
- "Would Christ be pleased with what is displayed in my video library, my magazine rack, or on my library bookshelves?"

- "Would Christ be pleased if He came and lived in my house for a week?"
- "Would Christ be pleased if He did what I did and went where I went?"

I can promise that the Christian will never regret one day of making Christ the center of his home.

∾

Checklist and Review

1. Christ must have the ___ in the life of any Christian.

2. The activity that should supercede any other activity of a Christian is ___.

3. Being a soul winner will bring ___ and ___ to a Christian.

4. In his life, a Christian must make ___ first; therefore, reading the ___ should be the first priority over reading newspapers, books, and magazines.

FOURTEEN

Handling Holidays

ONE OF THE more delicate matters a newlywed couple faces is that of how to handle holidays and special occasions with family members and loved ones who might not have the same beliefs and spiritual convictions. I believe much unnecessary heartache is incurred when there is no prior thought given to how these matters should be handled. Both sets of parents believe they know what is best concerning holiday plans and schedules when a young couple has their own personal wants. As a result, six adults are unhappy; when children are involved, usually the children are also unhappy. That situation is not right.

I believe it is impossible to please everyone at the same time. As Abraham Lincoln said, "You can please some of the people all of the time, and all of the people some of the time, but you can't please all of the people all of the time." Though Lincoln's quote is certainly not a Scriptural verse, it is an important practical idea. Still, I believe a couple can come closer to pleasing everyone if they take time to think about how to handle the delicate situations of the holidays.

Suppose you live within driving distance of both sets of parents, as I do. Where will you spend Thanksgiving Day, Christmas Day, New Year's Eve, or New Year's Day? How and when will you celebrate the birthdays and anniversaries of your various family members? These decisions are important matters that I believe an engaged couple should discuss before marriage. Having some brief, tender conversations before marriage about future plans with parents could greatly alleviate and reduce some of the fears and frustrations of parents.

When Cindy and I were planning to be married, I was concerned that my mother and father might feel some jealousy because I would now be living in the same community as my in-laws. Of course, I did not want my parents to feel threatened by the fact that I could see my in-laws on a weekly basis. At best, I would only see my parents on a monthly basis and maybe even less. So my wife-to-be and I counseled with her father about the situation. Of course, as I mentioned elsewhere, we decided that we would spend some time with my parents once a month by driving to Michigan where they live or by inviting them to visit us in Indiana.

Before we were married and when we were first married, we did not plan our holiday times. On some Thanksgiving Day holidays, we drove to see my family in Michigan, and then we drove back for an afternoon with my wife's family. On Christmas Eve, we drove from Indiana to Michigan to be with my family, then returned early Christmas morning to be with Cindy's family, and then back late Christmas Day to be with my family.

I have to admit that all of this traveling to see loved ones got to the point where holidays were almost to be dreaded. Finally, Cindy and I spent some time figuring out how to spend holidays in such a way as to make everyone at least content with our decision. Let me share what we ultimately decided. Perhaps our schedule would work in your situation. Of course, we have the added advantage that my parents live only two and one-half hours from us. My in-laws live 15 to 20 minutes from us, so we really have the best of both worlds. Basically, we can see either family almost any time we want to visit.

On Thanksgiving Day, a special service is held at First Baptist Church, so we spend our entire Thanksgiving Day with Cindy's parents. Likewise, we spend all of Christmas Day with my in-laws.

On Christmas Eve, our immediate family—Cindy, Jaclynn, Kenny, and I—spend the day together. We then spend New Year's Eve and New Year's Day, as well as three or four additional days with my family in Michigan. That time is like a little extended vacation with them. We have found that this plan works beautifully.

We try to celebrate our birthdays on the day by phone calls, or if possible with a visit, with a gift, and with a card. We are big about celebrating a special day on that exact day. My family, my parents, and my in-laws are all very content with this arrangement that we have now followed for many years. Our holiday times are predictable and comfortable for our traveling schedule.

᳁᳁

Neither Cindy nor I spend time we do not have running back and forth trying to please everyone and, as a result, actually becoming irritated with the situation. Perhaps your parents live a long distance from you, and you see them only as you can afford the finances for airline tickets. Be honest and explain the situation. If you will live in the same city as your family, decide in advance how often you will see them. Otherwise interference in the household by the in-laws could result.

❧

Checklist and Review

1. A special and unique problem that arises with a young couple concerning holidays is ___.

2. The best way to handle the holidays and family visits is to work out a ___ to which both the husband and the wife can ___ and stick to that ___.

3. It is impossible to please ___.

4. Unnecessary ___ comes when couples do not plan ahead concerning holidays and special occasions.

5. When holiday times are predictable, everyone can be ___.

FIFTEEN

Convictions and Standards

THE SEPARATED CHRISTIAN will have standards and convictions that, without prior planning, may interfere with family gatherings. Every engaged couple must be prepared to deal with family members who do not have their convictions or standards. Perhaps close relatives drink or smoke, watch inappropriate television shows or R-rated videos, or indulge in a behavior of another kind that is not appropriate. There are several ways to deal properly with the situation without alienating family.

1. **I would not sit in judgment or condemnation of family members.** A family has the right to run their lives; a Christian has the right to organize his life as he sees fit in the sight of God.

2. **I would not preach at them.** Scolding them, correcting them publicly, or even preaching a Bible sermon at them will not change them. Perhaps you could pay for a subscription to a Christian magazine or send some sermon tapes to which they could listen in the privacy of their house. It is not our place to confront them or judge them. They are adults who have made their choices.

3. **I would not condone their behavior.** Every person has a right to decide what goes on in his house. I, for one,

could not allow smoking in my house—not by my father, my mother, my sister, my father-in-law, my mother-in-law, nor any other person.

I have been blessed with godly family members, and I recognize just how blessed I am. Nonetheless, I am the man of my house and the head of my household, and I would not allow sins like smoking and drinking in my house because I believe they are Scripturally wrong. I will not allow my wife, children, or myself to be in that type of environment.

If I had an in-law, such as a brother-in-law or a sister-in-law who smoked and if they were visiting at my house, I would let them stay at my house. However, they would have to smoke outside. I would not scold them. I would let them know that I was very pleased that they were staying with my family. I would let them know I was delighted to be in their family, but I would be frank and firm and say, "In our house, we do not allow smoking. I know you smoke, and that is between you and your God. As long as you are under our roof, you will need to smoke outside. That is our simple rule. Therefore, we will live by the rules and be happy with each other."

I would not make a scene. I would not give my relative a sermon about the wickedness of smoking, the errors of his way, or the possibilities of cancer. I would love the person, but I would be firm about our rule. On the other hand, if I were to go to their house where they drink or smoke, I would have to decide if maybe it would be best to stay overnight at a motel, keeping in mind that I want to win my family not alienate them.

A young married couple may not be able to afford a stay in a motel, so they might want to plan their vacations so that they arrive early in the morning and stay late in the evening but not spend the night. If a couple feels like they must spend the night with relatives for the sake of peace, stay.

I do not believe that getting married gives a couple the right to suddenly become mean-spirited and say, "Now that we are married, we cannot condone those actions." If a couple decides to spend the night with non-Christian relatives, they must be prepared for some tense moments. If relatives decide to smoke or drink, it is their house, and they have the right to do as they wish.

One way to avoid difficulties is to invite the relatives to go elsewhere—perhaps bowling or miniature golfing. Perhaps playing some board games around the table or laughing together reliving good times may relieve tension.

If relatives decide to watch television, and it is something decent to watch without violating their Christian consciences, the couple might want to join them. If the program is something inappropriate, the Christian couple will need to leave the room. They might choose to read a good magazine or a book elsewhere.

If a relative says, "Why don't you watch this with me?" the issue does not need to be addressed. An acceptable answer would be, "When we are watching television, we can't talk, and we came here to talk and to be with you." The wise couple will approach the issue from the standpoint of wanting to be with the relatives, enjoying their company, and talking with them. By your not having a bad spirit about inappropriate television programs, the relatives will respond rather than react to missing a program. If a visiting couple seems angry or has a bad spirit toward them or the situation, the relatives will detect those bad feelings. They may well feel that the visitors are more interested in changing them rather than in spending time with them.

Always keep in mind that the reason for vacations is to spend time with loved ones. In order to do so, Christians just may have to be more creative. Take your relatives to places in their hometown which they may not have visited. For instance, in my hometown, I did not visit any of the so-called tourist attractions until I was dating my wife. Only then did I suddenly realize that my hometown had many fine places to visit, and Cindy became my inspiration to go to those places. Perhaps being married will inspire a couple to take their parents, family members, or loved ones to visit some of the local tourist attractions.

The relatives might enjoy using the upcoming visit as an excuse to have a completely different type of fun. After all, they may be tired of sitting around drinking and smoking, watching bad television programs, and grumping and griping about how rotten life is!

I beg you to use the head God gave you to think of some creative ideas and to plan a full day of activities—

- Drive to a U-Pick place to pick apples or blueberries or strawberries.
- Try patronizing a quaint restaurant in a scenic setting in the woods.
- Take a walk or drive through a game preserve to photograph birds.
- Collect stamps, baseball cards, coins, etc.
- Go to a used book store and browse the shelves.
- Play a board game like Monopoly.

Whatever you choose to do, use your creative imagination to keep away the tension or from having disagreements with relatives' habits and choice of lifestyles.

⌒⊙

The area where having convictions and standards gets most sensitive is when children arrive. When the lifestyles of relatives are contrary to what is taught and believed, parents will need to have some frank talks with their children about what they believe. At the same time, the parents need to stress how much the grandparents or the relatives are loved and how they are the best in the whole world. Explain that the loved one may have a little something in his life that is not perfectly right. Since nobody is perfect and since we cannot condone sin, we still love the person in spite of the wrong.

As Christians, we must not let someone's bad habit drive a wedge between loved ones. We must not let our children grow up thinking their grandparents are bad because they happen to smoke cigarettes. Please don't misunderstand me. I am a Baptist preacher, and I vehemently hate cigarettes and liquor. For many years, my grandparents smoked, and my grandfather drank. I am very grateful that my mother and father taught me to love my grandparents and to hate the sin rather than the sinner.

As a boy, I used to try to hide the cigarettes from my grandmother, and I tried to hide the liquor from my grandfather. Then I tried to keep them from finding the cigarettes and liquor that I had hidden. Of course, my tactics failed miserably. Thankfully, because of my parents' love, I grew up realizing that there is a way to separate a sin from a sinner, and I dearly loved my grandparents.

Thankfully, later they became much finer Christians as they began to attend church regularly. Both of them quit smoking and drinking. From watching my parents, I realized that patience and love can surely conquer so much more than bitterness and a mean spirit can.

More than likely, having strict standards will cause some tense moments. Therefore, doing some creative planning, having a full day of activities, maybe driving a few extra miles, and spending a little extra money will help build stronger relationships. I believe a couple who uses their imagination will accomplish a great deal more than if they show their disapproval with anger and an unkind spirit.

⚬⚬

Checklist and Review

1. When staying at a relative's house, it would be inappropriate to ___ or to ___ to them about personal convictions.

2. When staying in a relative's home, the Christian should never ___ in to their lifestyle.

3. When lifestyles are in conflict, the Christian couple should be ___ and courteous but ___.

4. List three simple solutions to unacceptable activities unsaved relatives may promote.

5. A Christian's standards and convictions do not have to interfere with family gatherings or with ___ family members.

6. To spend ___ with loved ones is the primary reason for a vacation.

7. In order to spend time with loved ones who have differing convictions, a couple may need to be very ___.

8. Bad habits can drive a ___ between a Christian and his loved ones.

9. Above all, when visiting your relatives, try not to have a ___ spirit.

SIXTEEN

Health: Diet and Weight

OCCASIONALLY IN MY marriage counseling, I deal with disagreements that arise between a husband and wife about their health, diet and weight, and at times, cooking. As I was counseling with one young couple, I said to the wife, "Do you know what your husband's favorite foods are?"

She truthfully answered, "No, I don't. I know a couple of them, but I don't know all of them."

"Do you know what foods he hates?"

Again she truthfully answered, "Oh yes, I know what foods he hates."

"Let me ask you another question. If he hates certain foods, and you know he hates them, then why do you prepare them for him?"

"Well," she replied, "I just feel those foods are a part of a balanced meal."

I said, "Your balanced meal is causing an unbalanced marriage."

I proceeded in the counseling session to present some ideas on how the couple could get along regarding food. I suggested that both make lists of their favorite foods and lists of the foods they do not like. I suggested to the wife that she should keep the lists and learn to cook well the items that he liked on his list. I recommended that she not prepare the items on his list that he did not like—healthy or not. "Why force him to eat something he does not like?" I asked. "He is an adult man, and if he doesn't like a particular food, he shouldn't have to eat it. You are not his mother!"

It is not the duty of the wife to make her husband learn to like new foods. Preparing what he enjoys eating is a simple way for any wife to show that she loves her man. It is also a simple way for a wife to know how to better love her husband.

Along these same lines of healthful eating and diet, I believe a wife ought to maintain within reason the weight she was when her husband fell in love with her. If he fell in love with a 135-pound woman, then she should strive by dieting and exercising to roughly maintain that 135-pound weight.

A husband and wife must be patient with one another. A spouse's weight may vary from time to time due to sickness or pregnancy. However, I still strongly believe that 90 percent of your married life you should maintain your reasonable ideal weight.

The same policy is true for the husband. If she fell in love with a 175-pound man, then he should likewise strive to maintain that approximate weight. There would be nothing wrong if an engaged couple decided to get into top physical shape, especially if either is a little overweight.

For a husband or wife to "let themselves go" in the name of a marriage vow and marital love is selfishness and laziness. To be perfectly honest, I believe it is wrong. A couple ought to be as disciplined and diligent to keep themselves as attractive and healthy and strong as they did when trying to win each other's heart and favor.

I believe a wife should learn to cook as healthy as her

husband's tastes enjoy. A wife probably should not force her husband to eat soy and tofu! Real men don't like that stuff anyway! Still, a couple should eat as healthy as possible.

I believe many ladies kill their husbands prematurely. Perhaps an early heart attack strikes because of the type of cooking a wife does. I believe it is a shame for a wife to cook improperly and take ten years from her husband's life causing him to forfeit his enjoying the children, the grandchildren, and even his wife for ten years longer because she did not want to learn how to cook in a little healthier way.

By no means can I give extensive helps, but common sense tells us that fried foods, excessive amounts of red meat, a lack of vegetables, an excessive use of oily snacks and greasy foods all lead to premature health problems and even early death. I know he may like the unhealthful types of food, and if he likes them, he should have some of them. Therefore, I believe an engaged couple should discuss the importance of taking care of themselves, beginning with proper and healthful eating.

A husband should not allow himself to become weak or obese just because he sits behind a desk and uses that sedentary job as an excuse to be overweight. He should exercise by doing sit-ups and push-ups, or walking, jogging, or weight training. I am thinking of an evangelist friend of mine in his late 50's who rises early to pray. The first thing he does every morning before he prays is about 100 to 150 push-ups. He has remained a strong man. Every husband should find something that he can do that will keep him in good health and shape. A husband should be a strong man in order to take care of his family all of his life.

Living by schedule and scheduling the proper amount of rest is vital. The couple should go to bed at the same time every night—together. Couples make a big mistake when one spouse goes to bed an hour or two before the other and is sound asleep when the other retires. That practice is not good for romance nor for building a strong marital bond.

Not only do I believe a couple should retire at the same time, but also I believe they should rise at the same time every morning. If one is an early riser, I believe the other one should learn to be an early riser. Both schedules should be adjusted to be in as much harmony and as synchronized as is humanly possible.

The Bible teaches that the two will become one flesh. *"And he answered and said unto them, Have ye not read, that he which made them at the beginning made them male and female, And said, For this cause shall a man leave father and mother, and shall cleave to his wife: and they twain shall be one flesh? Wherefore they are no more twain, but one flesh. What therefore God hath joined together, let not man put asunder."* (Matthew 19:4-6) Notice that the Bible did not say that two will become one spirit or one soul. The Bible said, *"one flesh"*; therefore, the flesh (the body) and the physical life should be in harmony as much as is possible.

A couple should eat as many meals together as possible. Those meals should be eaten together on time as much as possible. I cannot express how important a schedule really is.

A couple should enjoy recreational times together. Does the husband enjoy golf? If so, the wife should go along to drive the cart for her husband while he plays. The idea of a newly married husband going off to play golf with his friends as often as three or four times a week and leaving his wife alone is unwise. Both may have friends, but it is foolish to spend free time with friends and not with each other. Answer this for me: "Why are you getting married anyway?"

Wives: "Are you getting married because you need some of your husband's money?" That is a silly reason because it will cost more to be married than to be single.

"Are you getting married because you simply wanted to have children?" That is flawed thinking because the number one reason for marriage is companionship. Malachi 2:14 says, "*...Because the LORD hath been witness between thee and the wife of thy youth,...yet is she thy companion, and the wife of thy covenant.*" Marriage is God's answer for loneliness—companionship. God wants a married couple to be companions, friends, buddies, pals, and lovers.

I believe a couple should enjoy sports together, perhaps tennis, racquetball, bicycling, golf, long walks, even shuffleboard! Enjoying sports together can help a couple stay in shape together and be healthy together. The best way to reach those kinds of goals is to do them together.

Every couple should find something they like doing together. A couple should build their lives around each other. After all, isn't that the reason why a couple gets married?

⤳

Checklist and Review

1. Which is more important in a marriage relationship—a balanced meal or a happy marriage?

2. The weight a wife should seek to maintain in her marriage is the weight she ___.

3. A couple should be as aggressive in maintaining their appearance and attractiveness after marriage as when they ___.

4. A wife should balance his ___ and ___ when working on a menu for her husband and family.

5. A husband and wife should harmonize their ___ time and ___ times.

6. Scheduling the needed amount of rest and living by ___ is very important in keeping harmony in a marriage.

SEVENTEEN

Unresolved Conflicts

ONE OF THE handicaps brought into marriage is what I call the baggage of unfinished business or unresolved conflicts from previous years. Those unresolved conflicts will invariably reappear in marriage.

In our day and age, it is becoming more and more prevalent to find young ladies and even young men who have been molested, violated, abused, misused, or mishandled—even by loved ones. Either member of an engaged couple might have come from an abusive situation or a broken home. The disappointments of earlier years can bring some scars to a marriage that will eventually reveal themselves as cracks in the foundation of the marriage.

To keep these potential problems at bay, the couple must examine themselves and ask themselves two questions:

- Is there anyone you should forgive who has not been forgiven?
- Is there anyone you have wounded?

We have to forgive those who have hurt us just as God forgives, with an Ephesians 4:32 forgiveness. *"...forgiving one another, even as God for Christ's sake hath forgiven you."* To be sure, forgiveness does not mean making a a best friend of a person who has brought hurt. Neither does it mean going to that person and saying, "Let's become buddies and/or pals." Anyone who has caused hurt must be forgiven.

I believe a leading cause of all relationship breakdowns is bitterness. In my counseling, I have found bitterness falls into several categories.

- Bitterness arises because one spouse mistreats the children in the eyes of the other.
- Bitterness arises when finances are mishandled.
- Bitterness arises when one spouse mistreats the other's parents. He may dislike his mother-in-law or she may dislike her mother-in-law, and the door is opened for bitterness to enter.
- Bitterness arises when one spouse feels mistreated by the other.
- Bitterness arises because of something that happened in the past prior to the marriage, such as abuse by someone, parents' divorce, etc.

The embittered one has never dealt with the situation or received counsel. Consequently, he has never accepted the situation and the hurt, and he has never forgiven those who caused the hurt.

When we ask ourselves the question, "Is there anyone I have wounded?" we must examine ourselves and be objective. I have learned that the wound one person commits against another and is not forgiven will eventually be turned against a spouse. That unresolved conflict will eventually reveal itself in a marriage.

Marriage is a mirror that reflects each spouse's character level. That reflection and revelation is why so often, after many years of marriage, couples become very disillusioned with one another. Their marriage reminds them of their own failures. So often, a person will marry someone he perceives as a very sharp individual, in essence hoping that the person's strengths will make up for his own weaknesses. When he discovers that his weaknesses do not change because of his spouse's strengths, he becomes disillusioned and frightened that his spouse will be disappointed or frightened with him. Then he becomes bitter as he sees that mirror reflection of his weakness. Next comes disenchantment and sometimes even anger at the spouse who unknowingly is a constant reminder of his weaknesses.

That disenchantment and anger increases bitterness which will be a cancer that corrupts the marriage. Let me ask this question: Have you ever hurt someone? Have you brought heartache to someone for which you never apologized?

- Perhaps you stole from someone and never recompensed them.
- Perhaps you injured someone emotionally and never even said, "I'm sorry."

When someone wounds another, he often becomes bitter at that person because of the wound he has caused. I liken it to borrowing money. I have learned the hard way that whenever I loan money to a friend, invariably he stops paying me back. Then he gets angry at me and doesn't want to see me. *I* am the one who lost the money, but *he* is the one who will not speak to me. I have not only lost my money, but as a result of the loan, I have also lost my friend.

As a result of this type of scenario, I do not loan money to friends nor do I loan money I cannot afford to *give*. If a friend asks for a loan, I say, "No, I do not loan money." If I am able, I give the money to the person making the request and do not expect to be repaid. Money and loaning money to friends can cause bitterness more quickly than any of Satan's traps.

ೲ

More and more as I counsel young adults, I am finding the grown-up result of child abuse. If you were abused as a child, I strongly urge you to seek godly counsel from your pastor or a professional. The effects of childhood or teenage abuse can create major problems within an adult marriage. If the spouse brings the baggage of bitterness into his marriage, he is starting the marriage with a corrupting influence. It is far better to postpone the marriage and remedy the situation before getting married.

ᕙᕗ

Checklist and Review

1. A handicap carried from single life into married life that will eventually reappear is an ___.

2. ___ is the leading cause of all relationship breakdowns—not just of marriage.

3. A bitter person is bitter because he has never dealt with the situation causing his bitterness nor has he ___.

4. Marriage is a ___ that reflects each spouse's character level.

5. The strengths of one marital partner will not make up for the other's ___.

EIGHTEEN

The Wedding Day

L ET ME SHARE some important points to follow when considering the day for which the couple has waited.

　1.　**The wedding day is the bride and the groom's day.**
No, the wedding day is not a day for the mothers of the bride and groom; it is not a day for the sisters of the bride and the groom; it is the bride and the groom's day. Therefore I say, "Plan to enjoy your day! You are not performing for a crowd. You are not on display to put on a show. It is your day to enjoy one another."

Because the wedding day is for the bride and the groom, the wedding day needs to be planned so that everyone involved knows his role and so that everything involved is prepared properly.

The cake, though it is a delightful part of the service, is not the purpose of the day. Though they add a great deal to the ceremony, the bridesmaids and the groomsmen are not the purpose of the wedding day. Even the groom's tuxedo and the bride's gown are not the purpose of the wedding day. The bride and the groom enjoying the most significant day of their lives is the purpose of the wedding day!

Therefore, the bride and the groom need to be aware of each other. They need to notice each other. The bride and the groom need to love each other that day. They ought not to be so nervous about how they will stand on the platform that they forget why they are standing on that platform!

I have performed weddings where the bride and the groom were so worried about saying the vows after me that they did not even say them to each other. They became more worried about whether or not the ring was the right ring, and whether or not it was pretty enough that they forgot on whose finger it was going. I have seen couples get so worried about the fact that the groom, who did not like formal attire, would wear a boutonniere and tuxedo that they forgot why he was getting dressed! He needed to be reminded that the formal attire was for her! Sometimes a bride worries so much about how her hair will turn out on her wedding day that she forgets for whom she is wearing her hair—her groom!

The couple must realize that the wedding day is for them. That fact means the planning is up to the engaged couple. The planning is not for a mother who missed her wedding day because she chose to be married by a justice of the peace. Her daughter's wedding day is not a time for a mother to relive her lost dreams. Most definitely, the mother of the bride should be included in the planning, but this is not her wedding day. The wedding day is the only day in a Christian's life when one has the right to have it his/her way—it's the bride and the groom's day—exactly what they want, hope, and dream it can be.

2. The only thing that must occur on the wedding day is that the bride and the groom become husband and wife. Murphy's Law says, "Anything that can go wrong will go wrong." Inevitably, something will go wrong with the wedding plans or the rehearsal or the ceremony or the reception that follows. With numerous people with differing personalities joining together to be a part of a wedding and having only a couple hours of practice, something will go wrong. Someone will forget a part. Someone will get caught in traffic or by a train and be late. Someone might not arrive from out of town for the rehearsal. Someone might become ill. Someone, for whatever reason, might not be available for pictures.

Let me share one detail that went wrong at my wedding. Cindy and I had ordered a gorgeous, huge, elaborate cake as a backdrop on the platform of First Baptist Church of Hammond for the wedding ceremony. A very major problem arose concerning that beautiful cake which was to be a part of our decorations. The lady who was going to make the cake thought the wedding was the day after our actual wedding date. Understandably, with the mix-up of dates, the cake was not prepared. Thirty minutes before the wedding, my pastor (my future father-in-law) who was going to perform the ceremony came into the groom's room and said, "Jack, we have an emergency."

When he said, "We have an emergency," I thought that Cindy, my wife-to-be, had fainted or had a seizure or could not make it and that we would have to postpone the wedding.

Panic-stricken, I asked, "What is wrong?"

Brother Hyles said, "The cake didn't make it."

"Oh," I said, "I thought we had an emergency."

He said, "But this is your wedding day. We want everything to be right."

I happily replied, "The only thing that matters to me is that my fiancée makes that walk from the balcony, down the stairs, and up the center aisle to the platform. If I am there and she is there, please just make sure that you are there! I don't care who else does what or what else goes wrong. I am here today to get married. I am not here for a cake. I am not here for the pictures afterward. I am here to get married. That's all I want!"

Picture, if you will, a wheel much like a bicycle wheel. I want to compare that wheel to a wedding. On that wheel, the decorations, the attendants, the cake, the gifts, and all of the details pertaining to a wedding are peripheral. They are all outside on the rim of the wheel; the hub of the wheel is the bride and the groom getting married.

One way of preventing stress on the wedding day is to put the details on that day into the hands of a competent person. That person should be one who does not get out of sorts when problems arise. At First Baptist Church of Hammond, I am privileged to have Mrs. Elaine Colsten to care for the coordinating of weddings. She handles details well and does not get frustrated when unforeseen situations arise. Perhaps a sister, a sister-in-law, a friend, or an older lady in the church who is very good at planning social events could be consulted. That coordinator will prove to be a valuable asset as she helps to keep down costs and cares for all the little details on the wedding day.

All the bride needs to do is enjoy getting dressed, laugh with her attendants, have some pictures taken with friends, and get prepared for that grand entrance when she will present herself to her groom-to-be.

I always recommend to the groom that he choose a responsible best man, a man of good character who is dependable. The best man should take care of some of the details on the wedding day and delegate areas of responsibilities. By doing so, he will allow the groom to focus on enjoying his time with his groomsmen buddies and on getting dressed in his tuxedo. The groom should prepare himself psychologically, mentally, and spiritually for when his lovely bride presents herself to him.

Also, let me say at this point, choose bridal party members wisely. The wedding party can help make the wedding day everything the bride and the groom ever wanted, or they can create havoc. The couple should carefully decide how many and who should be a part of the bridal party.

3. The couple must not forget about those who helped them prepare for their wedding day. Though the wedding day is just for the bride and the groom, they ought not to forget about those who helped them get to a wedding day. The bride and groom should take time to remember people who have helped make a difference in their lives:

- Parents
- Grandparents
- Pastors
- The person who won them to Christ
- Sunday school teachers
- An older brother or sister
- A Christian school teacher
- A college faculty member

Any one of these persons may have provided insight and guidance at a critical and pivotal time of life. Perhaps the person stepped in and was used by God to keep the bride or the groom on the right path that ended in the wonderful crowning day of their marriage and in being in God's will. Often, people like grandparents who have made great contributions to the lives of the bride and the groom feel left out, even a mother or a father can feel slightly neglected.

Therefore, I recommend to the bride-to-be and to the groom-to-be to make brief but very personal phone calls to some of these people during the week of the wedding. Phone calls could be made to special people who are up in years who possibly cannot attend the wedding. A bride or a groom could call and say, "I just wanted to call you and say thanks a million for being there when I needed someone to show me the right way." That kind of acknowledgment is so appropriate.

During the week of the wedding or several days before the wedding day, both the bride and the groom should take time to write personal letters to their parents and to some special people, letting them know how grateful they are for their influence.

Those letters should say more than, "You are a wonderful person, and you helped me get to this day." Write about something specific that made a difference. The bride and the groom could write to the person who won them to Christ or to the pastor who preached a particular sermon when they were teenagers that changed their entire way of thinking.

Each should write an individual letter to Mom to tell her that she is the best mother in the whole world and why. Each should write Dad to let him know that he is the greatest dad in the whole world and why. The couple should thank their parents for their sacrifice of time and money, for providing a house and clothing, for arranging for piano lessons, for being spectators at the football games, for enduring basketball practices and piano recitals, for their taxi service, and most of all, for loving them and nurturing them. I can say from experience that parents are proud of their children. Parents need to feel that their children are truly grateful for all they received.

Don't just jot a note that says, "I love you, Dad. Thanks a million for all you do." This should be a lengthy letter carefully written two or three days before the wedding. As the groom places the envelope in his dad's pocket, he can honestly say, "Dad, there is something very important in that envelope. It tells you how much I love you. When I am on my honeymoon, please read it." That father may shed some tears, but he will know how much his son cared.

4. It is important for the bride and the groom to have an adequate amount of rest the week of the wedding. At the very least, on the day before the wedding, get some rest. It is not wise to stay up all night decorating the church for a pretty wedding day only to be exhausted and of no physical value on the honeymoon except to sleep. Not only is it unfair to each other to be exhausted the day of the wedding, it is just plain dumb. The couple hasn't taken the time to think through all of the ramifications of those actions.

Here they are planning the biggest vacation of their lives called a honeymoon. They will be going to some wonderful place for several days, perhaps a week, but they will be so tired from staying up late, they can't even enjoy their honeymoon. How silly! The night before the wedding, the bride and groom need to be in bed as early as possible.

When they arise the next morning, they need to spend some time with God. Their wedding day is symbolic of the day they will see Him in glory and be married to Him.

The morning of my wedding day, my dad and I played a round of golf. My dad knew it was a way of relieving tension, and we had a great father-and-son time the last couple of hours before we had to go to the church and get ready. Several times while we were on that golf course, I walked up to him, put my arm around his shoulder, and said, "I love you, Dad. What a grand life I have had being your son, and I have always loved it!" We got to be good buddies and pals in a special way for just a couple of hours that morning. So that a bride and a groom can have meaningful times like I had with my dad, they should not have last-minute plans of rushing to get something. As I mentioned before, a trusted coordinator can care for those last-minute necessities.

I always recommend to an engaged couple that they make sure days and weeks ahead of time that there is no need for last minute rushing. In my book, *Dating with a Purpose,* I have an entire chapter devoted to a checklist of plans of what to do and when to do it before the wedding day. Following such a checklist will enable a couple to pamper themselves on their wedding day!

5. On the wedding day, the bride and the groom should not eat foods that will disagree with them. I do recommend eating, but this day is definitely not the day for either to decide to try something new! Neither should say, "I am so nervous, I can't eat." No, both will live to regret that statement. The next day while on the honeymoon, one spouse could have a nauseated stomach or be ill which is unfair to the other.

6. The bride and the groom should make plans to arrive at the church with time to spare. They should plan to leave early enough that they still have plenty of time to prepare should a train stop on the tracks. The Hammond area is notorious for trains as well as for trains stopping and remaining stopped. Yes, trains still run on wedding days! If for some strange reason the car gets two flat tires, even with getting them fixed, the bride and groom should have planned enough time to be prepared.

7. At the wedding, the bride and the groom should pay particular attention to those who attend. While standing on the platform, maintain eye contact with as many people as possible. While the groom is waiting for his bride to appear, he should listen carefully to the solo being sung, and if he can, watch the person singing. If he is within eyesight, he ought to look at that person and realize, "This person is someone whom I love and whom my bride-to-be loves. We have asked him to be a part of helping us celebrate and enjoy this day." He should look at his grandparents being escorted to their places on the first or second row and love them in his heart. He can look at his friends who came and smile at them. What a wonderful time the wedding day is! Don't miss one moment of it!

I remind the bride and groom not to be so scared they don't realize who is there. The Lord willing, this moment is the only time a couple will have a wedding celebration. The groom should watch his bride as she walks down the aisle. As she is walking down the aisle holding tightly to her dad's arm, she should plan to say something sweet to her dad such as, "You're so handsome in your tux," or "I love you, Dad." She should be thankful to him for helping prepare her for marriage.

Then, when Dad gives his daughter to her husband-to-be, her groom should become her focus. She should look at her groom through eyes of love. Both should listen to the preacher as he talks. The bride and the groom should look into each other's eyes when repeating their vows. As they repeat them to each other, they should be aware of how holy and sacred the words are.

~~

Through the years, I have had scores of couples tell me that they went through their entire wedding day and did not even begin to realize what all happened. They were either too tired from activities the night before, or too weary from not eating properly and not taking care of themselves, or too nervous to notice the people. Their wedding day was spent as a ritual that they missed. How sad! A wedding doesn't have to be like that nor should it be. With proper planning, the day or evening can be truly unforgettable.

&

Checklist and Review

1. Because the wedding day is for the bride and the groom, it needs to be carefully ___ so that every person knows his purpose and his place.

2. The engaged couple is responsible for the ___ of the wedding because the wedding day belongs to ___.

3. One way to diminish stress on the wedding day is to assign the details of the wedding to a ___ person.

4. Both the bride and the groom should ___ themselves, psychologically, mentally, and spiritually for each other.

5. An important detail for the bride and the groom to care for on the wedding day is that they spend a few minutes writing notes to people who made a ___ in their lives.

6. Both the bride and the groom should be sure to get an adequate amount of ___ the week of the wedding.

NINETEEN

The Honeymoon

THE HONEYMOON IS an important, necessary part of the wedding day, even if it is a one-day stay in a modest motel. Therefore, I feel that I must address the subject of a honeymoon frankly and honestly. I advise a couple to measure the success of their honeymoon by being together. In this chapter, I will give the names of a couple of books to read in preparation for marriage and for the honeymoon. Regardless of what those books say, regardless of what any friends say, regardless of anything seen on television, regardless of what any magazine articles say about sexual enjoyment and marital love, the newlyweds should keep in mind that if they are pure and have never before enjoyed sexual romance, they will not be adept in the intimate marital relationship.

It does not matter how macho a man may believe he is or how feminine a lady believes she is, I can promise that it will take a while before both become familiar and comfortable with each other.

If the newlyweds are a pure Christian couple who have carefully and delicately guarded their purity through months and perhaps years of dating, the act of love requires some adjusting. Perhaps the couple attended a fundamental, separated Christian college with rules and standards requiring that couples not hold hands, kiss, or touch. The couple has obeyed the rules and stayed pure by following all of the dating rules. Suddenly, they are supposed to feel totally at home, comfortable, and act like "old pros" about being unclothed with each other! Trust me, that is going to be a big adjustment!

However, perhaps the bride or the groom or even both of them were promiscuous before they came together as husband and wife. Perhaps their past is not clean and pure, but they want to make this relationship right and proper. Even so, it will take time for a couple to get to know each other sexually and to be familiar, comfortable, relaxed, and at ease with one another.

I counsel a couple not to feel as though they must live up to some unusual physical expectation in order to be successful on the honeymoon. The whole idea of sexual love is extremely important to maintain a happy marriage. For many couples, what happens at that time of fulfillment is the release of an emotional buildup of anticipation. Even the joy of reality cannot quickly fulfill all the months and years of sexual waiting. Couples need to keep in mind that their bodies have been sexually prepared since early teenage years or even as early as fifth or sixth grade. For many years, a young person has been holding back that which marriage now allows a couple to release.

There is no way that a short honeymoon will satisfy or fulfill all of the couple's desires, dreams, or fantasies for sexual fulfillment. On the contrary, success in marriage means staying together, being happy together, loving one another, fulfilling one another's needs, and becoming the best of friends over a period of many years. I believe that success on a honeymoon means just being together.

When my wife and I got married, we got in a car alone for

the first time because we had not been allowed to have unchaperoned dates. Needless to say, both of our parents were very strict. In our car driving away from church, I looked at my new wife snuggling at my side, put my arm around her, and said, "Cindy, do you realize that everything from this point on is brand new?" As we were discovering the "brand new," we missed our exit to the motel because we were smooching and cutting up and having the time of our lives. We were teasing one another and reliving the wedding and laughing about some things that happened during the wedding ceremony and the reception.

As we drove toward our honeymoon destination, we had the time of our lives just being together. We didn't have to get to our motel room and wake up the next morning before we experienced something new! We were looking forward to a vacation in Hawaii given to us as a wedding gift by Russell Anderson, a Christian businessman who loved both of our families.

I can attest that Hawaii was a wonderful place to go on a honeymoon; and for us, going to Hawaii was a trip of a life-time. We had heard how beautiful our 50th state was, and when we got there, it was everything we had heard and more, and we enjoyed the beauty. We rented a little car, and I would guess we put 500 miles on that car driving on the island of Oahu. We went to the mountains, to every tourist trap, to every sightseeing spot, and to every restaurant we could afford. I know we made a million memories, and it seems like we took hundreds of pictures.

That wonderful honeymoon we enjoyed leads me to advise that the bride and groom plan activities to fill their days. This advice may sound funny because most couples have the mistaken idea that all they will want to do is stay in bed in the motel. Sexual love is certainly a wonderful part of marriage, but outside activities need to be planned; otherwise, the couple will not make hundreds of memories together on their honeymoon.

They ought to take advantage of every activity, such as horseback riding, canoeing, boating, fishing, swimming, hiking, or camping, they can while honeymooning. Tastes will be unique to the two of them, and there ought to be compromise. By all means, the newlyweds should want to do more together than just sleeping in late, watching television, and making love. Yes, some inactivity is fine, but it becomes very boring and not at all conducive to making memories. Planned activities make memories.

I have found that couples who date enjoyably and have a good dating life do things together when married. They don't just sit around and talk and talk and talk about nothing. They plan activities, and then they talk afterward about what they did. So, a honeymooning couple should plan activities and make memories. When they get home, they can talk about all the fun they had and renew their closeness as they talk again and again about the fun things they did while on the honeymoon.

One of the most important reasons why I believe a couple should have a counselor is so they can discuss intimacy. The bride should seek advice from her lady counselor about what to expect on the honeymoon night. The groom likewise should seek advice from a male counselor. If the bride and the groom have a background of promiscuity, they may have some negative experience. I believe there is no way to explain totally to a virgin what to expect. A couple should certainly have a general working knowledge of what will take place, what will change in their bodies, and what will take place so there is not a sudden surprise or disappointment in case the intimacy does not at first work out according to the text-books.

Sometimes a man gets very physically excited because he is not used to all of those new sensations. Those feelings can be almost overwhelming to him, and sometimes he is not able to fully control his physical appetites. When he cannot perform exactly like the textbook says, he may feel crushed. He may struggle with feelings of being less of a man, and then the wife may feel badly for him. As she tries to make up for his feelings of inadequacy, she may say kind things that make him feel awkward. Often, they both feel silly and self-conscious; their first sexual experience can almost become an embarrassment to them.

I have had many strong, robust, physically active young men tell me they became impotent for a day or a few days on their honeymoon because they were either exhausted or nervous or inexperienced. They were pure young men, and they shared with me that the act of marriage was almost overwhelming to their bodies. They were unable to release properly the wonderful ecstasy of joy they felt. Not being able to function properly is a severe blow to a man's ego. A young lady who does not anticipate that possibility could misunderstand that impotence as rejection. A young man who feels like he cannot properly satisfy his wife will some-times withdraw from her—not because he does not want to be with her but because of embarrassment, humiliation, and the fear of not being able to control his body.

Also, it is not uncommon for there to be a slight physical complication that might show up on the honeymoon that can very quickly be remedied in a doctor's office. If on the hon-eymoon, for some reason the couple is unable to consum-mate their physical love according to the books they have read and studied and according to what they had anticipated, they should not wait for weeks and weeks to seek help, thinking the problem will care for itself.

When the couple returns from the honeymoon, they need to go immediately to their Christian doctor, explain the situation, let him discuss the problem, and perform an examination. Many times a medical doctor's wise counseling and a simple procedure performed in his office can immediately allow newlyweds to enjoy romantic, physical love to the full degree that they had intended and hoped for before they got married.

These are just a few of the reasons why I believe a very detailed and frank talk with a person the couple trusts would be very prudent as the groom and the bride anticipate their first night. Of course, men should talk with a man, and ladies should talk with a lady about those matters.

When Cindy and I were looking forward to marriage, we read books that our parents advised us to read. Our pastor often mentioned how sad it is that engaged couples do not prepare for marriage. Doctors study as many as ten years to become specialized in a medical field. Most engaged couples do not read or study even five books on marriage in preparation for one of the biggest decisions in life they will ever make.

Let me share the titles of three books that might help a couple with romantic, physical love.
- *Intended for Pleasure* by Dr. Ed Wheat
- *The Act of Marriage* by Dr. Tim LaHaye
- *The Gift of Sex* by Clifford and Joyce Penner

These books may be purchased or ordered at a Christian bookstore. These books will give any couple a good understanding of what to expect and will help answer most questions a couple may have.

I believe every couple ought to read many books on marriage. There are hundreds of books on marriage being written today. When they go to their counselor, they should ask him for some titles of marriage books that he would recommend.

I would recommend that an engaged couple not read books dealing with the physical romantic side of marriage until three months prior to the wedding date. If a couple reads that type of book too soon, it can cause frustration and anxiety, and may well cause a couple to take some improper liberties with each other. I would recommend that couples set a date when they will begin reading that kind of explicit literature. Upon reaching that date, certainly the above-mentioned books would be an excellent start.

As the newlyweds begin their honeymoon, they should do the following:

1. Enjoy being alone together.
2. Enjoy learning each other's bodies.
3. Enjoy the vacation and sightseeing.
4. Talk freely and openly about the sexual experience.
5. Remember that really great sex for the two of them may take several months and even years to perfect.
6. Enjoy the journey.

∞

Checklist and Review

1. The intimate marital relationship will be a big ___ for newlyweds.

2. Staying together, being happy together, loving each other, fulfilling each other's needs, and becoming best friends can well bring about ___ in marriage.

3. ___ activities build and make memories.

4. To discuss intimacy is one of the reasons why an engaged couple needs to have a ___.

5. A engaged couple would be wise to read many books on marriage as one form of preparation for one of the biggest ___ in their lives.

6. A couple should wait until ___ before their wedding day to read books dealing with the physical aspect of marriage.

TWENTY

Transition Times

AS AN ENGAGED couple spends the last few months of their engagement together and as they spend the first few months of their married life together, they need to remember to be patient with each other. During dating days, the couple will transition from dates to work to classes to another date to work to classes, etc. Then as the wedding day approaches, the couple transitions into last-minute plans, changes, and preparations to the wedding day. Then comes the honeymoon, the return from the honeymoon, and the scheduled routine of work. During these many transitions, the couple needs to be patient with each other.

I believe one of the most difficult parts of married life is the minor transition from one activity to the next, such as when the husband leaves work to come home. Those first few minutes when he walks in the door can sometimes be the best or the worst time of an entire day. Another such time is the first five to ten minutes when getting up in the morning. What a husband and wife say to each other during this time is very important.

Our former preacher, Brother Hyles, wisely taught that a couple should wake up at the same time and then spend five or ten minutes just holding and cuddling each other and beginning the day with an embrace. This five or ten minutes allows the couple to transition out of the sleep mode and into the wake-up mode.

Another time of transition for a couple is leaving the house to go to church. Many a family spends an entire ride to church fussing, arguing, yelling, scolding, and then putting on pious faces when they walk into the house of God. That home-to-church transition time can be a difficult time.

Another important time of transition is after meal times. In our home, we have a time of prayer together after the evening meal to help the transition. These little five-minute times of transition can make or break a marriage as a couple moves from activity to activity and from place to place. A couple will notice these transitions much more when children come onto the scene. For instance, five minutes from the time they are picked up from school to come home is a crucial time. Their minds are still on school, and they will seem distant. It takes an artist, a gifted, wise parent, to bring that child out of his "school" shell, to be patient with the child, and to allow the child to be alone in his silence. I cannot stress how important transition times can be in creating harmony in the home.

A harsh word spoken during a transition time is much more severe than a harsh word spoken when a couple has been together for a lengthy time. Therefore, I highly recommend planning the times of transition. For instance, before the husband gets home, he should plan what he is going to say when he walks through the door. He should prepare in his heart and mind for his wife. It might even be a good idea for him to call his wife and say, "I am on my way home. I'll be home in ten minutes."

When the wife knows he will be coming home, she should stop what she is doing, spruce herself up, splash on some perfume, change into a fresh dress, slip into high heels, and greet him at the door with a loving hug and kiss. A wife's preparing for those first five or ten minutes when he is home will do more to enhance marriage than a good meal that she has been preparing for two or three hours.

All of life is a series of transitions—going from duties, responsibilities, and activities. Those little in-between times are where so many drop the ball and make a big mistake. Love is a constant probing, a constant testing. Jesus said to Peter, "...*lovest thou me more than these?*" (John 21:15b) Even our Saviour probed the depth of love of his disciples to see if it was genuine or real and to see what depth of love they had.

A couple will probe and test each other's love. In the greatest commandment of all, Jesus said, "...*Thou shalt love the Lord thy God with all thy heart, and with all thy soul, and with all thy mind. This is the first and great commandment. And the second is like unto it, Thou shalt love thy neighbour as thyself.*" (Matthew 22:37–39) I believe what Jesus was saying was, "You said you loved Me. Prove it. Convince Me of that love."

A couple's love for each other will go through some incredible tests over the duration of the marriage, whether it be 30 years or 60 years. They shouldn't be afraid to have their love tested. Nothing is wrong with that testing, but as it is tested and probed, they need to make sure they are committed to letting their spouse find in them a heart of genuine and patient love.

❧

Checklist and Review

1. A couple should always remember to be ___ with each other.

2. Some of the most difficult times in a new marriage are times of ___.

3. Your times of transition should be ___.

4. All of ___ is a series of transitions.

TWENTY-ONE

A Wedding Checklist

Each section of this checklist contains an overview of what needs to be done to have a successful wedding day. This checklist will enable the couple to stay organized and will take them step-by-step through all of the preparations necessary for planning the perfect wedding.

SIX-NINE MONTHS BEFORE THE WEDDING
- ☐ The man should seek permission from the lady's parents to become engaged.
- ☐ Have a formal engagement with a ring.
- ☐ Place engagement announcement with pictures in local papers.
- ☐ Set up pre-marital counseling appointments with pastor or counselors.
- ☐ Obtain a list of recommended books on marriage from pastor and begin reading.
- ☐ Bride's father should determine budget amount for wedding.

FOUR-SIX MONTHS BEFORE THE WEDDING
- ☐ Decide on the type of wedding you desire. This decision will be determined by your gown, the men's attire, formal

or informal reception, decorations, and the number of
attendants. Keep your budget in mind.

❏ Set the date, time, and place.
❏ Select your attendants.
❏ Considering both families, make up your guest list.
❏ Choose your wedding gown.
❏ Choose your bridesmaids' dresses and men's attire.
❏ Secure the services of your church wedding hostess or a
bridal consultant, if possible.
❏ Plan your future home furnishings.
❏ Buy your wedding rings.
❏ See your pastor.

THREE MONTHS BEFORE THE WEDDING

❏ Plan your reception. Make arrangements with a caterer (if
planning a formal reception) and secure a location for
your reception.
❏ Order the cake.
❏ Plan your music.
❏ See your florist and order your flowers.
❏ Select a photographer and confirm the date.
❏ Order your invitations, announcements, and stationery.
❏ Set the date for rehearsal.
❏ Plan your wedding trip. Make all of the necessary reser-
vations.
❏ Begin shopping for the trousseau.
❏ Have your mother and mother-in-law confer with each
other concerning their gowns.
❏ Secure birth certificates from the court house in the
county in which you were born.
❏ The bride should consult with doctor about marriage and
health questions.

TWO MONTHS BEFORE THE WEDDING

- ❏ Plan a method of recording your gifts.
- ❏ Make arrangements for the display of gifts.
- ❏ Keep up with thank-you notes as each gift arrives.
- ❏ Address the wedding invitations.
- ❏ Consult your fiancé about the rehearsal dinner plans and the guests to be invited.
- ❏ Make appointments for medical and dental checkups.
- ❏ Make an appointment with your hairdresser.
- ❏ Arrange a final fitting of your gown.
- ❏ Select gifts for the bridesmaids and the groom.
- ❏ Set the date for your bridesmaids' luncheon (if one is planned).
- ❏ Arrange housing for out-of-town guests.
- ❏ Arrange transportation to the church.
- ❏ Have a formal portrait made, if desired.

ONE MONTH BEFORE THE WEDDING

- ❏ Mail the wedding invitations.
- ❏ Endeavor to have friends who are planning showers for you to do so now.
- ❏ Buy necessary items for your new home, and make any moving arrangements.
- ❏ Set up a gift display, if you plan one.
- ❏ Set aside everything you will wear on your wedding day, and keep it together.
- ❏ Check on bridesmaids' apparel and be sure ensembles are complete.
- ❏ Send wedding announcements and glossy prints to the newspapers.
- ❏ Make final arrangements with your caterer, baker, reception hall, florist, photographer, and wedding consultant.
- ❏ Arrange place for bridesmaids to dress together.

☐ Plan seating arrangements for the rehearsal dinner and the reception, if necessary.

☐ Attend parties in your honor.

☐ Have your hair styled as you desire for your wedding day. Take along your headpiece to be sure it will fit.

☐ Appoint a special aide to help you with details and unexpected events.

☐ Review books on the physical aspect of marital love.

TWO WEEKS BEFORE THE WEDDING

☐ Apply for your marriage license with your fiancé. Be sure you both take your birth certificates with you.

☐ Send the rehearsal dinner invitations.

☐ Assign attendants' tasks, such as taking gifts to your home, removing keepsakes from the church, retrieving the cake top, guest book, etc.

☐ Make a final check of bridesmaids' dresses and accessories.

☐ Select gifts or write checks for pianist, organist, soloists, custodians, P.A. workers, nursery attendants.

☐ Select a special gift or personal expressions of gratitude for parents and pastor.

ONE WEEK BEFORE THE WEDDING

☐ Be sure you are current with all thank-you notes.

☐ Pick up your marriage license.

☐ Collect your trousseau items and have them ready to pack.

☐ Be aware of your health needs, and don't neglect to eat correctly.

☐ Confirm necessary reservations.

☐ Relax! Spend some time with your family.

❏ Change name and address on your legal documents, i.e., driver's license, social security number, etc.

ONE DAY BEFORE THE WEDDING
❏ Pack your luggage.
❏ Leave your honeymoon itinerary with your parents or someone responsible, should you need to be contacted.
❏ Arrange for someone to check your home occasionally while you are away.
❏ Make a final check of your luggage and go to bed early.

THE WEDDING DAY
❏ At last the day has arrived! Calm yourself, pamper yourself, relax, and enjoy your wedding day!
❏ Share a breakfast or a cup of coffee with your parents.
❏ Speak to your fiancé/fianceé on the phone. (My traditional upbringing does not allow for the groom to see his bride before the wedding.)
❏ Make a call or two to a friend, a special convert or a bus kid, or a close relative unable to come to the wedding.
❏ Don't neglect your Bible and your Saviour on this day that symbolizes His love for you.

AFTER THE WEDDING
❏ Be sure to send a photograph and wedding announcement to local newspapers.

CONCLUSION

Marriage Is Good!

In conclusion, I will reiterate what I say to every couple I counsel, "You are in this marriage for the long haul. You will disappoint each other. You will frustrate each other. Twenty years from now, you will realize the person you married has changed considerably. In many ways, he will not even be like the person you married, but neither will you. Be patient with yourself, stay faithful to God, and may God's richest blessings be upon your marriage and upon your wedding day.

"May God bless you with children. My hope and prayer is that you will show them by example and teach them that marriage is wonderful. I want your children to say someday, 'My parents are the happiest couple I know. Their marriage has taught me to love and respect the institution of marriage. Their marriage has taught me that marriage is good and that people can work out their differences. Because of my parents, I believe the greatest and deepest love is the love between a husband and a wife.'

"God bless you."